The Power

Toughness

A Practical Guide to Improving Your Self Discipline, Gain Self Confidence, and Build Mental Resilience For Success

Peter Graham

©Copyright 2021 Peter Graham - All rights reserved.

The content contained within this book may not be reproduced or transmitted without direct written permission from the author or the publisher.

Under no circumstances will any blame or legal responsibility be held against the publisher, or author for any damages, reparation, or monetary loss due to the information contained within this book. Either directly or indirectly. You are responsible for your own choices, actions and results.

Legal Notice:

This book is copyright protected. This book is only for personal use. You cannot amend, distribute, sell, use, quote or paraphrase any part, or the content within this book, without the consent of the author or publisher.

Disclaimer notice:

Please note the information contained within this book is for educational and entertainment purposes only. All effort has been executed to present accurate, up to date, and reliable, complete information. No warranties of any kind are declared or implied. Readers acknowledge that the author is not engaging in the rendering of legal, financial, medical or professional advice. The content within this book has been derived from various sources. Please consult a licensed professional before attempting any techniques outlined in this book.

By reading this document, the reader agrees that under no circumstances is the author responsible for any losses, direct or indirect, which are incurred as a result of the use of the information contained within this book, including but not limited to, errors, omissions or inaccuracies.

Special Bonus!

Want this Bonus Book for FREE?

DETOX YOUR HABITS:
Stress Free Habit Building For Better Productivity

Get FREE, unlimited access to it and all of my new books by joining my Fan Base!

SCAN W/YOUR CAMERA TO JOIN!

Thank you for choosing to buy *The Power Of Mental Toughness*. If you enjoyed reading this book then please consider leaving a review on Amazon. I personally read all reviews and look forward to your feedback. Please scan either the U.S or U.K barcode below to take you directly to the review page.

U.S

U.K

Table of Contents

The Power of Mental Toughness 1
Table of Contents 5
Introduction 6
Part 1 The Royal Marines Commando Mindset 12
Chapter One: Mental Toughness is Cultivated 13
Chapter Two: Self-Discipline is King 34
Chapter Three: Fear – More Friend Than Foe 48
Chapter Four: Courage – Staying True to Yourself and Your Values ...67
Chapter Five: Unshakable Self-Confidence 90
Part 2 The Game Plan 115
Chapter Six: The Amateur Mental Toughness Training Program 116
Chapter Seven – Pro Mental Toughness 148
Chapter Eight – Elite Mental Toughness 170
Conclusion 187
References 193

Introduction

Have you been making resolutions that you don't follow through on? Do you wish to change your bad habits but you feel enslaved to them? Are you living a life full of guilt for not being the person you always wanted to be?

If you answered yes to any of these questions, then this book is for you. If you are going to treat this as just another book you read and forget about, then nothing will change. This book can change your life, but you have to be the one to make the choice to change in the first place.

You can't sit by the sidelines and wait for life to happen to you. You have to jump in the tempestuous waters of life and fight to get what you want.

We live in a world that has become too soft. It has become okay for people to get offended and hurt about everything under the sun. Instead of focusing on developing a thicker skin and a more indestructible personality, people want the easy way out by blaming others and life's circumstances.

If that sounds like you, then it's time for a change. The world doesn't owe you anything. Success is never served on a silver platter to those who want to be bystanders in the theatre of life. Success is the prerogative of warriors – those who have toughened their minds and bodies with discipline.

You can't achieve anything worthwhile in life without self-discipline and emotional control. If you are going to allow yourself to be controlled by your whims and emotions, then you will end up where most people spend their entire lives – in a cesspool of mediocrity.

Greatness is achieved by those who are determined to do what no one else is willing to do. You can't achieve anything extraordinary in life by exerting an average amount of effort. If everything about you is average – your personality, your actions, your mindset – then, your life will be average.

People think that successful people are lucky. From my own experience as a former Royal Marine and a successful entrepreneur, I know that luck favors those who persevere no matter how tough the going gets. Those who sit at the pinnacle of greatness are simply willing to persist longer than anyone else. They believe in themselves

Introduction

even if the whole world doesn't have faith in them. They keep their sights fixed on their goals with a single-minded focus. No matter how many times they fall down – they get up every single time and charge ahead towards their goals with even greater zeal and determination.

You have the same capacity for greatness as the best athletes, businesspeople, marines, and anyone else who has done things that the masses can only dream about. The question is: are you ready to believe in yourself?

Transformation begins the moment you realize that you are 100 percent responsible for everything that is happening in your life right now. Most people remain stuck in that cesspool of mediocrity because they are not willing to take responsibility to change themselves and their lives.

The life you are living right now is a result of the person that you are. If you have been average so far, then, it shouldn't be surprising that your life is average. If you think this is all that you are capable of, then you are right. If you believe you have been born for greatness, then you are also right. Whatever you convince your mind to believe becomes your reality. There are no exceptions to this rule.

I joined the Royal Marines when I was 19. Until that point, I had been average at everything I did. When most people think of marines, they imagine someone brawny and muscular. I was nothing of the sort. I was a skinny kid who was still figuring out his place in the world.

The training that I underwent brought out the extraordinary person that had been hiding behind that lanky frame all that time. I soon realized that the body can do anything that you can convince your mind of. The limits of your body are the limits of your mind. Over time, I have also realized that the limits of our imagination are the limits of our life.

How do you think that it is possible for a person to earn a million dollars in a day while another struggles to make ends meet? It has everything to do with mindset and the value that you create. If you are doing something that can easily be done by many other people, then your work won't be valued as much. When you become a brand in yourself, that's when you have value that can never be replaced.

You also have to start believing that you are capable of creating and receiving the things that you desire most. It doesn't matter whether the object of your desire is a million dollars in the bank account, a fit and healthy body, a great marriage, or anything else. The rules of the game remain the same. It all begins with mental toughness!

You can't discipline your body without first regimenting your mind. Without self-discipline you can't build a routine for success and

Introduction

routine is the key to lasting success. You become what you think and do regularly. To become an extraordinary person you have to think like an extraordinary person. You have to be willing to do things that no one else does. This could mean waking up at 3 am when the whole world is asleep, saying no to a fun party when you must stay home to master your craft, sacrificing your evenings to take a course that would give you an edge in your career, or maybe just waking up early enough to show up at the gym every morning.

You must understand one thing. Nothing -- and I mean nothing -- comes for free in life. If you want anything worthwhile, you have to be willing to pay the price. The price isn't necessarily a monetary one. The price of greatness is self-discipline, hard work, consistency, perseverance, and a willingness to go the extra mile when everyone else has given up.

Are you ready to change your life?

I'm not offering you a miracle here. You won't achieve anything by simply reading this book. What I am giving you is the roadmap for success. If you apply it fervently and passionately to your life, then you will create the life you have always wanted and become the person that you have always wanted to be.

The Power of Mental Toughness

Every moment of life is a choice. Average people follow the path of least resistance doing what is the easiest moment by moment. Extraordinary people are intentional with their time. They understand that time is the greatest asset they have and it is a consistently depreciating asset.

They don't have even a moment to waste because they are so utterly and wholeheartedly obsessed with their goals. Even when they are relaxing they are intentional with it. This means they may choose to meditate or go to the spa instead of watching mindless television. They are devoted to becoming a better version of themselves and they're willing to do whatever it takes to achieve their goals.

If you are ready to do whatever it takes and promise to never give up no matter how tough the going gets, then I am here to tell you that this book is going to change your life.

In the first part of the book, I will share with you everything that you need to know about cultivating a winner's mindset. In the second half, we'll discuss how to practically cultivate mental toughness the Royal Marine way.

You won't be the same person by the end of this book. That's a Royal Marine's promise to you. If you're ready, then let's get going!

Introduction

Part 1
The Royal Marines Commando Mindset

Chapter One: Mental Toughness is Cultivated

Pain is temporary. It may last a minute, or an hour, or a day, or a year, but eventually it will subside and something else will take its place. If I quit, however, it lasts forever.

- Lance Armstrong

Contrary to popular belief, mental toughness is not something that some people are blessed with and others are not. We are all born with the same capacity for greatness. The only difference lies in the fact that some people choose to realize their potential in life while others prefer to let life happen to them.

What exactly is mental toughness?

Mental toughness is what you are employing when you want something so bad that you'd do anything to get it. It doesn't matter what kind of odds are stacked against you, failure is an option you can't afford to consider. You're ready to do or die. The very idea of giving up doesn't exist anywhere in your mind.

Why Some People Have it and Others Don't

Are you saying you don't have that kind of mental toughness?

Well, here's a scenario for you: There's a fire and the person you love most is still inside the building. Either you run inside to save them or you watch the building burn knowing they're inside and will die. What would you do? I bet you wouldn't care how dangerous the situation is and how many odds are stacked against you. You would jump into the fire to save the person you love most. Won't you?

If you have that kind of mental toughness under such extraordinary circumstances without even thinking about or analyzing it, then why wouldn't you have that same grit and determination for pursuing your goals? The fact that you become an extraordinarily mentally tough person in one situation proves that you have the capability of being that person at other times, as well.

If you want to be successful at anything, you must want it more badly than your next breath. Failure shouldn't be an option. Each temporary setback should only increase your motivation to go after what you want just like how a rubber band snaps with greater force when it is pulled to its limits.

What makes some people great is the fact that they persevere when others give up. They believe that where there's a will, there's a way. No matter how many times they fall down, they never fail to get up. They have no time to feel sorry for themselves or blame others for their challenges. They see each challenge as a hurdle they have to jump in order to achieve the next level of greatness.

Mentally tough people are constantly focused on solutions. They know that there's a way out of everything. Finding the way and emerging victorious at the other end of every dark tunnel is what builds character. Character is not built by sitting at home watching TV and eating potato chips. It is built by fighting with all your might every single day of your life in the arena of life.

When Muhammad Ali was asked how many sit-ups he does in a day, he answered, "I don't count the sit-ups. I only start counting when it starts hurting because they're the only ones that count. That's what makes you a champion."

What makes one person a champion and another one an average Joe is their ability to tolerate pain. The average person lives with the pain of regrets, constantly making excuses for why they can't have what they desire. The champion, on the other hand, endures the pain of hard work and perseverance. He does what is needed even when it is painful to do so. He doesn't just do what needs to be done – he puts his heart and soul into it.

The champion is so committed to his goals that he is willing to put everything he has and everything he is at stake to get what he wants.

The Key Words are Consistency and Commitment

It's no big deal making New Year's resolutions but the question is how many people follow through on their promises to themselves?

The difference between champions and everyone else is that champions don't do what's needed only when they feel like it. They get out of bed even when their body is aching and it is freezing cold outside. They show up at training even when every muscle in their body is revolting in unison.

In the first phase of our training in the Royal Marines, we were taught to have extremely high standards for ourselves in every area of life. Hence, we were trained in personal hygiene, housekeeping, and etiquette. The rigorous military training schedule was never accepted as a good excuse for not making our bed properly every morning or being immaculately dressed when reporting to our seniors.

We didn't do these things when it was convenient. We maintained these standards for ourselves even when it was extremely hard to do so. That's why Royal Marine training changes your life forever. As they say, "Once a Royal Marine, always a Royal Marine." (The Royal Marines Charity, n.d.) Being a marine is a lifestyle and not just another job. You are expected to set the bar really high for yourself. Every time you achieve a new goal, you set that bar even higher. *Easy* is a word that doesn't exist in the dictionary of a marine. It's a grueling but intensely rewarding life.

I want to emphasize here that mental toughness is built with habits, not through motivation. You can't wait for motivation to strike or you would spend your entire life being a bystander. To be mentally tough, you have to study the habits of successful people and incorporate those habits into your own life.

Once you commit yourself to those habits, you don't give yourself any room for an exit. You do what's needed every single day whether you are feeling like it or not. Average people are too focused on their feelings. They allow themselves to be ruled by their emotions. They'll do something when they are 'feeling like it' or they won't do something because they aren't 'feeling like it.' If you want to achieve an elite level of mental toughness like a marine, then you do what's needed, not when it's easy or convenient, but when it needs to be done. Period.

Royal Marines Ethos

Mental Toughness is Cultivated

The Royal Marine ethos has 3 key components: the commando mindset, the commando values in life, and the commando spirit.

The Commando Mindset

In the Royal Marines, we are trained to "be the first to understand; the first to adapt and respond; and the first to overcome." (The Royal Marines Charity, n.d.) This doesn't mean that all of us are technically or practically the first ones to understand, respond to, and overcome the different situations we find ourselves facing. Instead, it's about mastering the mindset of the first-responder.

While working as marines, we are constantly exposed to intensely dangerous situations. In such situations, we can't wait for someone else to take the lead. We have to take the lead and be willing to do what's necessary in that situation. Instead of looking to safeguard ourselves, we put ourselves in the line of danger to protect our oppo.[1]

If you want to develop the commando mindset, then you have to become internally motivated instead of looking for external commands or demands. It doesn't matter what your line of work is, you can become a first responder by doing what other people are too lazy or unmotivated to do. You don't wait for your boss, colleague or client to

---

[1] Oppo: A close friend. The opposite number of a two man team; a system used to ensure maximum effectiveness in military activities.

demand that something be done. Instead, you go out of your way to deliver more than what's expected of you.

Excellence is never achieved by doing average work. It's a prerogative of those who are willing to constantly go above and beyond. Always set your standards higher than what's expected in a particular situation, and don't give yourself any leeway to fall short on it in any way.

Don't wait for someone else to take up the difficult work. You claim it for yourself and allow your character to be built by overcoming challenges. Every time you do something that compels you to move beyond your comfort zone, you are growing and expanding; you are becoming extraordinary. As you increase your capacity to do difficult things, your pain threshold also rises. What used to be excruciating eventually becomes easy. This is the key to greatness and the secret of champions.

Be a first responder to your fears and procrastinations. The things that scare you the most are the ones that you really need to do first. This is where your highest potential for growth lies.

The Commando Values in Life

These are the values that the commando is expected to live by both on and off duty:

Mental Toughness is Cultivated

- Excellence: Strive to do better.

- Integrity: Tell the truth.

- Self-Discipline: Resist the easy option.

- Humility: Respect the rights, diversity, and contribution of others (Logan, 2019).

As commandos, we are expected to strive for ***excellence*** no matter the circumstances. We have to often navigate unfamiliar terrain and deal with harsh climatic conditions. The stakes are extremely high and the challenges can appear insurmountable to an untrained mind. No matter what the nature of external challenges are, the Royal Marines culture involves demanding the very best out of oneself. We keep the bar extremely high for ourselves even if our lives are at stake.

I believe that ***integrity*** is another aspect of excellence. You can't aspire for excellence without integrity. Having integrity implies being able to speak the truth or/and do the right thing despite the consequences it might attract. It's following your conscience when no one is looking.

Having integrity and striving for excellence requires great ***self-discipline***. It's very tempting to choose the easy option but as commandos, we are trained to opt for what would bring the best results and not what would make our lives easier. Self-discipline can come only by mastering delayed gratification. It's that choice in the morning between an hour in the gym or a piece of chocolate cake. If you choose the first one, you will go through your entire day feeling like a champion. If you fall for the temptation of the latter, then you will find yourself writhing in guilt and self-loathing.

Despite all their achievements, commandos are expected to practice *humility* and be respectful to others at all times. If you want to achieve greatness, then you must maintain what is known as the beginner's mind in Zen Buddhism. A person's downfall begins the very moment he thinks he has achieved something or has become someone. I'm not saying that you shouldn't be proud of yourself but there is a thin line between confidence and cockiness.

Master the art of keeping your ego aside. Be humble and always willing to learn. Just because you know how to do something doesn't mean that there can never be a better way to do it. Keep an open mind – be coachable. Champions are life-long learners. They never stop growing and becoming better. The potential for growth is infinite and it's the project of a lifetime that never ceases.

The Commando Spirit

Harboring the commando spirit is all about:

- Courage - Get out front and do what's right.

Mental Toughness is Cultivated

- Determination - Never give up.

- Unselfishness - Oppo first; Team second; Self last.

- Cheerfulness in the face of adversity - Make humour the heart of morale (Logan, 2019).

The marines face extreme situations of life and death on a daily basis. They are expected to act with extraordinary courage when difficult and potentially life-threatening situations pop up. It's quite incredible to be part of a team where everyone has the determination to be the very best version of themselves and are ready to do whatever it takes to make every mission a success.

Commandos aren't focused on their own survival or well-being. They are guided by the spirit of unselfishness – their goal is to protect their team even at the cost of their own life. And they do it with a smile on their face. Without cheerfulness, it would be very easy to succumb to doom and gloom in the face of extreme adversity.

From now on, I would like you to face every situation with courage. This doesn't mean you won't feel the fear – the whole point is to feel the fear and do what needs to be done anyway. Be determined to give your very best every day – not to please anyone else but as a sign of self-respect to yourself.

At the same time, it is easier to give up when your goals are centered only around yourself. Hence, you need a bigger motivator – something that goes beyond your own self in order to remain internally motivated at all times. For instance, a mother who has to feed her children would do anything in the world to provide for them as compared to someone who only has to care for themselves.

I am not saying that you need to be married or have kids to become completely internally motivated. The chances of you sticking to your goals are higher when you are doing it for a reason that goes beyond your own self. Maybe you are doing it for the greater good of the community or even humanity at large.

While pursuing your goals with single-minded determination, don't forget to remain cheerful. Never allow any challenge to bog you down. There is a solution for everything even if you can't figure it out at the moment. Instead of focusing on how big a problem or challenge is, why not make light of the situation by finding the humor in it! Now, you may say your problems are no laughing matter. But the question is: does the excessive seriousness and negativity create any constructive outcomes? You'd be more likely to find a solution when you take things lightly.

Mental Toughness is Cultivated

Here's a favorite quote of mine from Dawn Gluskin: *Don't take life too seriously! Nobody gets out alive anyway. Smile. Be goofy. Take chances. Have fun. Inspire.*

Get Comfortable Being Uncomfortable - If it Was Easy, Everybody Would Do it

Mediocrity loves comfort! The reason why most people are average or mediocre is that their desire to be comfortable is stronger than their desire to succeed. They don't want to take chances or do difficult things. They do what is easiest and most comfortable in any situation.

Everything you want lies just outside your comfort zone.

- Robert G. Allen

You can never achieve greatness by being or doing what is just 'good enough.' Champions do things that no one else is willing to do. When we watched Kobe Bryant perform on the basketball court, some of us thought he was special or different. The ordinary person never asks, "How did Kobe Bryant become the person that he was? What does it take to be a Kobe Bryant?"

There are those people who think of the wins on the basketball court as isolated events guided purely by luck and stardom. They fail to realize that what happens on the court is the culmination or the grand finale of what goes on behind the scenes. It is easy to say that some people are just lucky or special and completely dismiss the endless hours of training they undergo to become the person that they are. Next time, when you come across someone you really admire, don't just gush with fandom. Instead, ask yourself, how can you incorporate the same qualities in yourself?

You can never become an extraordinary person by doing ordinary things. The secret of success lies in your daily routine. A lot of people would think that the daily life of a champion is utterly boring and repetitive. Repetition and endless hours of honing one's craft is what it takes to become a champion.

To become a champion, you'll have to master the art of delayed gratification. Watching TV, eating potato chips, partying with your friends are all things that bring some kind of immediate gratification but these things can never lead to true fulfillment. True fulfillment can be achieved only when you are sacrificing your TV time for learning and becoming a better person than who you were yesterday.

You'll have more self-respect and self-love when you are determined to feed yourself a healthy diet. To become a champion you'll have to rearrange your priorities. I'm not saying that you should never go partying with your friends. There's a time for work and there's a time for celebration. You must earn all your celebrations!

Be Careful with the Company You Keep

There's a lot of truth in the old adage 'misery loves company.' You become like the people with whom you choose to spend your time. Jim Rohn, one of the world's most famous motivational speakers once said, "You are the average of the five people you spend the most time with."

If you are spending time with people who have no higher aspirations and are content with a life of mediocrity, then that's who you will become whether you like it or not. The reason why the Royal Marines is such a life-transforming experience is that we get to live and breathe in an extraordinary environment of excellence 24/7.

I'm not saying that you should ditch all your old friends. I'm suggesting that you become more conscious and intentional with your time. Other people's mindsets and energies are constantly rubbing on to ours. This is why when you go to a self-improvement seminar, you feel extremely motivated while you are there. When you come back home it is hard to retain that same level of determination and motivation that you felt while you were at the seminar.

It really helps to have an accountability buddy – someone with similar goals who is willing to hold you accountable. I would suggest that you start networking with people who think like you and who are as committed to excellence as you are.

In the age of the internet, everything is just a click away. If you can't physically be with an extraordinary person, then you can certainly watch their videos and read books about their life or their works.

For starters, I would suggest that you pick one person whom you truly admire and study their life. While researching and studying, you will realize that you are starting to become like that person.

Every time you really admire someone, ask yourself what qualities they have that you would like to incorporate in yourself and then do just that. To become great, you need to be in the company of great people!

Wet and Dry – Train Like a Marine

Royal Marine Commandos are as fit as Olympic athletes and that's because they train like elite sportsmen. A typical day involves at least 3-4 hours of grueling physical training. We are required to push our bodies and minds to their limits.

One of the toughest training is what we call the 'wet and dry routine.' On exercise, we keep two sets of rigs or gear. We get soaking wet throughout a day of intense training. At night, we put on our dry clothes and get inside our warm sleeping bags only to have to wake up in the middle of the night for sentry duty in our wet clothes. Of course, no one wants to get up in the middle of the night and show up for duty

Mental Toughness is Cultivated

in uncomfortable wet clothes. We train our minds to do what's best instead of what's easy or comfortable. I am not suggesting that you train yourself by doing a wet and dry routine at home. What I am suggesting is that you incorporate the core mindset that gives us the strength to train like this.

One thing that almost all successful people have in common is the fact that they start their day early. They wake up before everyone else in their household does. You will be amazed by how much more you are able to get done by simply starting early and by waking up before everyone else.

Another thing you can do to train yourself in mental toughness can be to take a brief cold shower as soon as you wake up. It's amazing what a spritz of cold water early in the morning can do for you. It gets you wide awake and also makes you realize that your body can bear anything if you can convince your mind about the same.

Now, if you aren't already extremely fit, a cold shower in the morning might not be for you. You can start waking up early, though. Shrug off laziness. Get out of bed as soon as the alarm clock buzzes. If you are one of those people who keep putting their alarm clock on snooze, then you are starting your day on a note of failure and disappointment. You failed to do the very first thing that you had scheduled for the day – waking up at an appointed time.

This failure avalanches into your entire day because you start out by not feeling good about yourself. You can have self-confidence only by showing up for yourself every single day. Don't allow yourself to make excuses. Hold yourself up to extremely high standards.

Why You Will Never Succeed Without Mental Toughness

It really is all about the survival of the fittest whether in life or on the battlefield. By fitness, I don't mean just physical fitness. Physical fitness is extremely important but mental toughness is even more important than that.

To achieve greatness, you have to be mentally resilient. If getting knocked down once is enough for you to bail yourself out of the game, then you are just not tough enough. Being resilient means you spring back from every setback and failure in the fastest manner possible. You don't sit around and brood over how bad things are. You analyze what you could have done differently and what you can learn from your mistakes.

You take the wisdom and drop all regrets. If you haven't succeeded yet, then that means it's not the end yet. Don't accept failure. Keep beating at the door until it unhinges and breaks open. You can't have that kind of grit and determination if you are one of those people who keeps a plan B.

Mental Toughness is Cultivated

You make a plan and you trust that you are going to succeed at it. You will keep working hard until you succeed – whatever it takes to get there or whatever time it might require.

There's no other option – success is the only choice you give yourself. Every failure should motivate you to charge faster and stronger towards your goals. There should be nothing in this world that can dissuade you from pursuing your goals with single-minded determination. Each setback is like a little hurdle that you have to jump to elevate your skills and become a better person than who you were yesterday. With every passing day, you are getting closer to success even if the evidence of the same isn't apparent yet. Success is your one and only choice – it can never elude you for too long!

Chapter Summary

- We are all born with the same capacity for greatness. The only difference lies in the fact that some people choose to realize their potential in life while others prefer to let life happen to them.

- Mental toughness is what you are employing when you want something so badly that you'd do anything to get it. It doesn't matter what kind of odds are stacked against you, failure is an option you can't afford to consider. You're ready to do or die.

- Mentally tough people are constantly focused on solutions. They know that there's a way out of everything.

Mental Toughness is Cultivated

- What makes one person a champion and another one an average Joe is their ability to tolerate pain. The average person lives with the pain of regrets, constantly making excuses for why they can't have what they desire. The champion, on the other hand, endures the pain of hard work and perseverance.

- Mental toughness is built with habits and not through motivation. You can't wait for motivation to strike or you would spend your entire life being a bystander.

- It doesn't matter what your line of work is, you can become a first responder by doing what other people are too lazy or unmotivated to do. You don't wait for your boss, colleague or client to demand that something must be done. Instead, you go out of your way to deliver more than what's expected of you.

- Having integrity and striving for excellence requires great self-discipline.

- Face every situation with courage. This doesn't mean you won't feel the fear – the whole point is to feel the fear and do what needs to be done anyway.

- Mediocrity loves comfort! The reason why most people are average or mediocre is that their desire to be comfortable is stronger than their desire to excel and succeed.

- You can never become an extraordinary person by doing ordinary things. The secret of success lies in your daily routine.

- If you are spending time with people who don't have higher aspirations and are content with a life of mediocrity, then that's who you will become whether you like it or not.

- One thing that almost all successful people have in common is the fact that they start their day early. They wake up before everyone else in their household does. You will be amazed by how much more you are able to get done by simply starting early and by waking up before everyone else.

- Being resilient means you spring back from every setback and failure in the fastest manner possible. You don't sit around and brood over how bad things are. You analyze what you could have done differently and what you can learn from your mistakes.

Chapter Two: Self-Discipline is King

Personal self-discipline is the No.1 delineating factor between the rich, the middle class, and the poor.

– Robert Kiyosaki

Nothing worthwhile can ever be achieved without exercising self-control and self-discipline. The problem with average people is that they lack the discipline to take consistent action towards their goals. They join the gym on a whim but fail to show up after a few days of going there regularly.

Being self-disciplined means acting with consistency. You don't wake up to go to the gym only on the days that you are feeling like doing so. You do it every day without fail whether you are feeling up to it or not.

You don't stop working when you are feeling tired and exhausted. You stop only when you are finished. You don't show grit and determination on some days and let it fizzle on other days. You abide by your core values every single day despite the circumstances.

It's not starting strong that matters so much but staying strong that makes all the difference. Most people start out strong and then lose their motivation in just a few days. You need to have a vision for the person that you want to become and what your ideal life looks like. Emotional motivation is the key here. When you imagine your ideal life, do you feel a powerful surge of emotions or not? If the answer is no, then your goals are not providing enough motivation for you.

You need to have a clear mental picture of how you would feel, who you would be, and what you would be doing if you had already achieved your goals. The clearer this picture is, the more motivated you are going to be.

Every time a temptation crops up in your periphery, you pull up this vision in your mind's eye and remind yourself why you are doing what you are doing. Self-discipline is easier to practice when you know why you must keep yourself disciplined right now. For instance, if your goal is a fit and lean body, and you have a very clear vision of how you would look and feel if you were already that person, then it would be a lot easier for you to say no to that greasy hamburger.

Self-Discipline is King

Self-discipline is developed through self-knowledge. You need to know who you are, what you truly want out of life, what motivates you, and what tempts you. For this, you have to spend time alone in contemplation and analysis.

If you are one of those people who are constantly bombarding their system with sensory stimulation, then you can't ever become self-disciplined. You know the type – they need the TV playing in the background constantly or listening to brain-dulling 'music.' These are the people who can't be alone for a moment. They are afraid of silence. It's almost like they are afraid to hear the voice of their soul if the external world around them went silent.

Don't be such a person. Cut out sensory stimulation, and instead opt for silent contemplation. Regular self-analysis is the key to consistent self-discipline.

Why Self-Discipline is Different from Mental Toughness

Mental toughness is a mindset and an attitude that you acquire. It is shaped through the adoption of values like resilience, determination, courage, overcoming adversity, and assuming full responsibility for every aspect of your life.

Self-discipline is a tool that you use for acquiring greater mental toughness by habitually doing what is necessary to get closer to your goal(s).

Mental toughness is finding the extra strength and willpower to get over the line of a marathon when every muscle and bone aches in your body. Self-discipline is every single day of training before that. It's the saying no to a Friday night party so that you can get up early in the morning to train. It's the yes to getting out of a warm comfortable bed to go running every single time you are supposed to, irrespective of the weather or how you are feeling inside.

Mental toughness is saying no to a takeaway meal of fast food after a long day's work when the last thing you want to do is fix a healthy and wholesome meal for yourself. Because of your self-discipline and commitment to eating healthy, you cook at home anyway.

Mental toughness is having the grit and determination to open another door every time one door closes on you. Self-discipline is finding the keys to unlock it.

Self-discipline is action-oriented while mental toughness is attitude-oriented. Self-discipline gives you the ability to say no to that which will lead you astray and yes to that which will take you closer to your goal.

Mental toughness is the cumulative result of all those times you failed and then picked yourself back up again. It's about all the extra responsibilities you put on yourself and the courage that inspired you to carry them out successfully. Mental toughness is what you have acquired – self-discipline is the means for acquiring it.

You become tougher and more resilient every time you get yourself to do something that was once beyond your pain threshold. Mental toughness is your ability to bear pain – it's a bar that you constantly keep raising for yourself as you take on new challenges and explore new horizons. Self-discipline keeps you on track by making sure that you show up every day to fulfill the promise that you have made to yourself and/or to others.

Mental toughness and self-discipline are siblings. They go hand-in-hand. You need both of them in equal measure to be successful at anything in life.

Why You Can't Rely on Motivation Alone

Motivation is a fickle and unreliable friend that can't be relied upon to get anything done. If you are one of those people who are forever waiting for motivation to strike you before you can make your next big move, you are likely to remain in a state of limbo forever.

Replace motivation with decisiveness.

Instead of waiting for motivation to strike you, make a choice. You know what your goals are: now you have to choose to take the next step whether you are feeling motivated to do so or not.

Once you start taking decisive action, you'll automatically start feeling motivated to do more. You don't show up only on those days when you are feeling motivated. Instead, you show up when you make the choice to do so – and that should be every single day.

If you aren't taking firm consistent steps in the direction of your goals every single day, you are wasting your life. I know that sounds harsh but you need to know and accept the truth before you can do anything about it.

There is no perfect time to get started. If you think that someday circumstances will be perfect for what you want to do, then you are gravely mistaken. Life is always going to be imperfect. No matter how careful you are, you will certainly make mistakes. In fact, one of my mentors told me once that the only way you can really learn something is by making a lot of mistakes.

Self-Discipline is King

There is no perfect choice, no perfect day, no perfect circumstance. All that you have is this very moment – the now. The only question that matters is are you moving closer to your goals at this very moment or away from them?

You need to create a schedule for yourself and then make the choice to stick to it. This is how Franz Kafka managed to produce so many great works while holding a day job. He wasn't sitting around waiting to be inspired. He followed a daily schedule wherein he wrote for a few hours every single night (Clear, 2014).

You do what you need to do – put all feelings aside. If you allow your feelings and emotions to rule you, then you will continue living a life of mediocrity. Use your emotions to visualize the fulfillment of your dream. Keep your vision set on your goals by having internal emotional motivators. But NEVER allow your emotions to get the better of you.

Emotional control is the key to success. If you can keep your emotions in check no matter what the circumstances are like, you will be more likely to succeed. Do you think the marine commandos will be successful on the battlefield if they allow their emotions to control them?

You have to keep your focus on what needs to be done and not on the emotions that are constantly rippling inside you. As we discussed in the previous chapter, the best way to do this is by retaining a cheerful disposition and seeing the humor in every situation.

Delaying Self-Gratification - Exercising Self-Control

All successful people have mastered one superpower – delayed gratification. They don't do what makes them feel good right now. They do what makes them feel good in the long run.

Winners embrace hard work. They love the discipline of it, the trade-off they're making to win. Losers, on the other hand, see it as a punishment. And that's the difference.

– Lou Holtz

This means instead of gorging on that slice of chocolate cake right now, you choose to eat steamed vegetables. While that might not feel like a lot of fun in the moment, it will lead you to your ideal body. Willpower and self-control are absolutely essential for delaying gratification.

If you can say no to all the immediate temptations that derail you from your goals, then you will definitely achieve your goals eventually.

The Marshmallow Experiment

Self-Discipline is King

There was a famous study that was published in 1972 known as The Marshmallow Experiment (Wikipedia contributors, 2021). In this study, children between 4-5 years of age were given one marshmallow and told that if they could resist the temptation of eating it, then they would be given two marshmallows later on.

Some kids immediately ate the marshmallow while others managed to resist for a while but eventually they caved in as well. Only a very small group of children was able to resist eating the marshmallow. Later on, through follow-up studies, it was discovered that these kids were more successful in life than their peers.

The question is: Are some people born with a superior ability to resist temptation and delay gratification?

The answer was discovered by another group of researchers at The University of Rochester. They divided kids into two groups. One group of kids was offered reliable experiences while another group was given unreliable experiences (Kidd, 2012).

Both groups were promised something bigger and better than what they were originally given. The promise was fulfilled only to one group while it wasn't to the other one. The kids in the former group were able to train their minds to see delayed gratification as something positive since they were eventually rewarded for their patience and self-control.

The latter group had no reason to trust that they would eventually receive something bigger and better so they consumed what had been given to them.

Hence, the skill of delayed gratification is not necessarily something that you are born with but it's definitely a trait you can develop and acquire.

Reward Yourself Regularly

The best way to train yourself in self-control and delayed gratification is by rewarding yourself regularly for exercising self-discipline. This could mean if you manage to get yourself to the gym 6 days a week, on the seventh day you would have a cheat day. The idea is to set small goalposts for yourself with targets that you can easily achieve. When you do make it to your goal, reward yourself by doing something you truly enjoy.

This way you will train your brain to understand that it is worth waiting for things. Be sure to always keep your deadlines realistic. The biggest mistake people make is that they start big instead of small.

For instance, if you haven't exercised in a year, you can't set your goal as going to the gym twice a day 6 times a week. That's downright unrealistic. Even if you did manage to get to the gym for a few days, it will cause you to burn out and give up because your body and mind don't have the capacity to handle that level of training.

You must ease yourself into your new routine. If you haven't exercised in a year, it's enough if you can go to the gym for half an hour. The point is that you want to get started right away. You don't want to wait for the perfect set of circumstances – no postponing it till that date in the future from when you are planning to follow an immaculately clean diet.

You do whatever you can right now. Imperfect efforts are better than none at all. If you can't get to the gym for half an hour, then go there for 15 minutes. If that also feels impossible, then go out and take a walk for 10 minutes. If you are struggling to do even that, then get up from the couch and walk on your stairs.

There's always something you can do in the moment no matter how big your final goal is. You want to get started immediately instead of someday when the stars will be aligned just perfectly. Changing your life is something you do one step at a time.

What is it that you really need to do but have been postponing? What is the big picture goal? What can you do right now to get started with working towards this goal?

I want you to write down the answers and then do something about it – right now!

You don't become a champion by reading about how to be a champion. You become a champion by doing the type of things that champions do. This is your time to get started. Start small but stay consistent.

Self-Discipline is King

Chapter Summary

- Nothing worthwhile can ever be achieved without exercising self-control and self-discipline.

- Being self-disciplined means acting with consistency. Go to the gym even on the days that you aren't feeling it.

- Self-discipline is developed through self-knowledge. Know who you are, what you truly want out of life, what motivates you, and what tempts you. For this, you have to spend time alone in contemplation and analysis.

- Self-discipline is action-oriented while mental toughness is attitude-oriented. Self-discipline gives you the ability to say no to that which will lead you astray and yes to that which will take you closer to your goal. Mental toughness is the cumulative result of all those times you failed and then picked yourself back up again.

- Instead of waiting for motivation to strike you, make a choice. You know what your goals are now so take the next step whether you are feeling motivated or not.

- Emotional control is the key to success. If you can keep your emotions in check no matter what the circumstances are like, you have a better chance for success.

- All successful people have mastered one superpower – delayed gratification. They don't do what makes them feel good right now. They do what makes them feel good in the long run.

- You do whatever you can right now. Imperfect efforts are better than none at all.

Chapter Three: Fear – More Friend Than Foe

There is only one thing that makes a dream impossible to achieve: the fear of failure.

- Paulo Coelho

Everyone experiences fear – there are no exceptions to this rule. The only difference is in the way we deal with fear. Those who choose a mediocre life see fear as something bad that must be kept away at all times. Successful people see fear as an indicator of what they really need to do. It's often the things that we fear doing the most that carry the greatest capacity for growth.

By avoiding fear you are choosing to live small. Expanding your horizon means acting on your fears instead of avoiding them.

What is it that you fear most? What is the worst possible scenario you can imagine if you followed through with what you fear doing?

More often than not, the consequences are never as bad as we imagine them to be. However, the cost of not taking action is always very high. Instead of focusing on what you fear, why don't you think about what you are missing by not doing the things that you fear most?

It is better to try and fail than to have never tried at all. There is no shame in failing. Failure is only a temporary experience. Things always change for the better if you persist long enough.

The other reason why most people never do what they want to do is that they are afraid of what other people will think. They live in this box where the opinions of others matter more to them than their own integrity and self-respect.

I want to urge you to care more about what you think about yourself. You are the only person in the world whose opinion should truly matter to you. If you love and respect yourself, then no one's negative opinion or judgment will affect you. By following your heart and doing what your intuition tells you to do, you will enhance your self-esteem which will lead to even greater success in the long run.

What if I Fail? Consequences for Not Starting

Michael Jordan, one of the greatest basketball players the world has ever seen, famously said, "I have missed more than 9,000 shots in my career. I have lost almost 300 games. On 26 occasions I have been entrusted to take the game-winning shot, and I missed. I have failed over and over and over again in my life. And that is why I succeed."

Steve Jobs got fired from the very company he had co-founded. Despite being fired from Apple, Jobs went on to create a new company, NeXT, which eventually acquired Apple. Apple reached new heights of success once Jobs was leading it again. (*6 Stories of Super Successes Who Overcame Failure*, 2014.)

In her 2008 Harvard Commencement address, J.K. Rowling said:

> So I think it fair to say that by any conventional measure, a mere seven years after my graduation day, I had failed on an epic scale. An exceptionally short-lived marriage had imploded, and I was jobless, a lone parent, and as poor as it is possible to be in modern Britain, without being homeless. The fears that my parents had had for me, and that I had had for myself, had both come to pass, and by every usual standard, I was the biggest failure I knew... So why do I talk about the benefits of failure? Simply because failure meant a stripping away of the inessential. I stopped pretending to myself that I was anything other than what I was, and began to direct all my energy into finishing the only work that

mattered to me. Had I really succeeded at anything else, I might never have found the determination to succeed in the one arena I believed I truly belonged. I was set free, because my greatest fear had been realized, and I was still alive, and I still had a daughter whom I adored, and I had an old typewriter and a big idea. And so rock bottom became the solid foundation on which I rebuilt my life. You might never fail on the scale I did, but some failure in life is inevitable. It is impossible to live without failing at something unless you live so cautiously that you might as well not have lived at all – in which case, you fail by default (2008).

I can add countless stories here of some of the greatest men and women who have experienced massive failures in their life yet they are remembered for their greatness and achievements. You can never succeed without experiencing failures first.

If you are too afraid to start, then you will never learn anything new. After all, when you are doing something new, you are going to start out by being terrible at it first. You become exceptional at something only by learning from your mistakes. The more mistakes you make and the more resilient you are, the faster you'll learn.

Fear – More Friend Than Foe

Of course, any smart person will also learn from other people's mistakes. You don't have to make all the mistakes yourself to learn from them. Find someone who is already successfully doing what you want to do, and learn from them. This would prevent you from making a lot of mistakes. Even then, it is inevitable that you will err at some point.

Failing at something is not the worst thing that can happen to you. The worst thing you can do to yourself is to accept any temporary setback as a permanent failure. Failure is final only if you give up and decide to not try again.

The famous motivational speaker Les Brown has a book titled It's Not Over Until You Win. The title says it all. Winners never accept defeat. They keep fighting until they win the game – it doesn't matter how many setbacks they encounter along the way or how many times they fall down. They keep working hard until they get what they want. If you can find that level of persistence, perseverance, and determination in yourself, then I can assure you the Universe will bend over backwards to reward you with everything you have so far only dreamed of.

Nothing is impossible. All things are possible for those who try and those who never give up. The only real failure lies in never starting.

If you haven't started yet and you keep procrastinating on when you'll begin, you have already failed.

Let me give you a task: make a list of all the things that you would accomplish if you did get successful at what you want to do. Once the list is ready, read it over several times. That's exactly what you are losing by idling away in inaction!

You are the architect of your destiny. Henry Ford famously said, "Whether you think you can, or you think you can't -- you're right." You can do anything that you set your mind to do. Believe in yourself more than you believe in the idea of failure. If you can cultivate a formidable spirit wherein no setback can prevent you from chasing after your goals, then I can guarantee you that success will come knocking at your door. It may take a while but it will definitely come.

Why Failure is the Best Thing That Can Happen to You

If you are still in a state of limbo whether to act on your dreams or not, I am here to tell you that failure is the best thing that can happen to you. It is not something to be dreaded but a wonderful thing that should be embraced.

Imagine – when you were little you got a new bike. As you were learning how to ride it, you fell many times. You got bruised and battered. Every time you fell down, it did hurt. You mustered all your

Fear – More Friend Than Foe

strength and got back on the bike. One fine day, a miracle happened – you could ride the bike! You found that perfect balance that kept the two wheels moving together in perfect sync while you remained perched on it. That moment of victory felt so good! You were over the moon – it was as if you had grown wings and could fly like a bird.

Now imagine if you had never gotten back on that bike after the first time you fell down. Would you have ever learned to ride a bike?

There's a learning curve involved with everything in life. You don't become amazing at something when you are doing it for the very first time. When you were learning how to drive, you had to concentrate on so many things. For a while, it seemed impossible that you will ever be able to drive as effortlessly as you see other people doing it.

Then over time, something changed. Now, you can eat your breakfast, comb your hair and drive at the same time (not that I advise doing these things while driving). The point is that even the most seemingly impossible things become easy over time.

The learning curve helps us develop mental toughness. Every time you recall something difficult that you accomplished through sheer persistence and determination, you know you can use the grit you have acquired to achieve even greater things in life.

Nothing is impossible for the one who keeps trying. Every time you encounter a failure, know that you are developing greater mental toughness. In the same way that you lift heavier weights to become stronger, you have to take on new challenges in life to become a stronger and more successful person.

Most people prefer to live an easy life. They choose the path of least resistance. Hence, they never achieve greatness. Big success comes with big risks and even bigger failures. Bruce Lee said, "Do not pray for an easy life, pray for the strength to endure a difficult one."

Don't contract your horizon by choosing to live small and easy. Expand your consciousness by choosing to do that which is difficult and challenging. Become best friends with your fear because the things that you fear the most are the things that you need to do the most.

Those are the things that will take you to the zenith of greatness. It's not the destination that matters so much but the journey that you take to get there. Character is built along the path to greatness. Even if you lose everything after acquiring great success, you can rebuild your life because you have developed the mental toughness to do so.

Overcome Defeatist Self-Talk

The most important person you can ever talk to is your own self. Whether we are conscious of it or not, every single one of us is constantly talking to our own self – not in a vociferous way but quietly inside our minds through thoughts.

Unfortunately, most of the time, these thoughts that pop up in our minds are negative. The negative comments we heard from our parents and teachers eventually become part of our own subconscious. While that critical parent or teacher may not be around to say something like, "You really think you can do that?" it is now your subconscious that is saying all these things to you.

All of us have to overcome these negative thoughts as almost no one has had a perfect life where we weren't criticized in our childhood. Of course, the degree to which we experienced it differs from person to person. For some people, it is easier to overcome these negative thoughts and for others, it is very hard. Either way, if you are determined to change, then you CAN change. Nothing is ever impossible if you are willing to remain persistent and do the work.

Become Self-Aware

Self-awareness is the most important key to success. Successful people exercise control over their mind and emotions instead of being controlled by them. You need to constantly remain aware of the type of thoughts and emotions you are experiencing.

The next time, your mind says something like, "You can never do anything right," pause for a moment and watch that thought. Don't let it consume you and swallow you into a whirlpool of negativity. Instead, detach yourself from your mind. Observe that this thought has occurred in your mind and then analyze it objectively.

Think about all the times you did do things right. Most likely, the number of times that happened was significantly higher than the number of times you didn't do things right. Remind yourself of all your successes and accomplishments. If you are struggling to find them, then ask someone close to you what they think are your greatest successes and accomplishments.

Remain self-aware and detached from your thoughts at all times. Of course, this is not easy but that's what becoming successful requires – you have to be intentional with everything including the thoughts that you choose to mull over. Don't hold on to thoughts that aren't there to serve your highest good or that lead you astray from your purpose and goals.

You don't have to be perfect – you just need to be persistent with being self-aware.

Transform the Negative Self-Talk

When a thought begins to really bother you, it's time to work on transforming it. Let us go back to the example of your mind saying to you, "You can never do anything right." You mulled over this idea and you reminded yourself of all the times you did things right, now we must create a new affirmation.

Flip the negative self-talk around to create a new empowering statement such as, "I am outstanding at everything I do." It's very important that you don't think of this statement only in your mind: write it down. Writing does something to our brain – it helps the subconscious imbibe the ideas at a much deeper level.

You can also write down your negative self-talk and then create a positive counter-statement for each one. Once you have the positive statements, burn the negative self-talk. There is something ritually transformative about setting fire to your self-destructive and defeatist thoughts that have been put to paper. Try it out – I can guarantee you that you'll feel lighter and better.

Don't Moan – Be Grateful

Gratitude is the most powerful form of prayer. Any situation can be transformed from a negative to a positive one through the power of gratitude. The next time you are feeling unhappy about having to do something, shift your attitude. Instead of thinking, "I have to clean the house – it's such a pain," say to yourself, "I get to clean the house – I am so blessed."

The first sentence makes you think that the task of cleaning the house is a burden. The second one helps you realize how blessed you are to have a house to live in and wonderful things to surround yourself with. By cleaning the house you are getting a chance to express your gratitude to the space that nurtures you and keeps you safe.

This same mindset can be applied to every aspect of life. Never do anything while thinking of it as a burden. Spend some time thinking about how doing it is blessing your life. There is always something to be grateful for no matter how grim things may look on the surface.

Every experience is there to make you stronger, provided you are ready to embrace the lessons it contains. You can recognize the blessing very easily by always replacing "I can't," "I don't want to," or grudgingly said, "I have to," or "I must," with the empowering statement, "I get to."

Fear – More Friend Than Foe

Control Only What You Can

Most of the stress and tension we experience is because we are constantly worrying about things we can't control. Even worse, we worry about things that haven't even happened yet. I want to suggest that you shift your way of thinking.

Every time you find yourself getting worried about something that may happen in the future, pause for a moment and think about the opposite coming true. Heaven and hell are within your mind. You can create a living hell for yourself by constantly dwelling on the negative or you can experience the serenity of heaven by focusing on that which is pleasant and uplifting.

When things are indeed not going the way you would like them to, it's important to detach yourself from your immediate reality. Instead of focusing on what you are experiencing, think about yourself as a character in a movie. Everything is happening to the character in the movie and not to the real you. This sense of detachment will help you in remaining more pragmatic and practical no matter what you are facing.

Another important tool that every successful person has in their arsenal is visualization. Whether it is footballers or wealthy business people, they visualize a positive outcome long before they set foot on the football pitch or enter the meeting room.

Neville Goddard, one of the greatest spiritual teachers of the century, introduced the idea of living in the end. You visualize the outcome that you truly desire and live as if that's your reality. No matter what happens in the middle, you remain faithful to your end goal – the final vision that you are carrying in your mind's eye. Eventually, everything (even the negative things and setbacks that happened along the way) that happens in the middle would help pave the path to reach your desired end.

Even if you don't believe that would actually happen, it still feels good to keep your focus on what you truly want and live as if you have already received it. You most surely will receive it anyway because the outer world is a reflection of the inner world. Living, in the end, will prevent you from getting flustered by the undesirable things that are happening at the moment.

Give it a try – if nothing else you will feel more peaceful. It would be easy to remain unfettered by temporary setbacks and failures. Think of it this way: If you know how a movie is going to end, you wouldn't get agitated or unnerved when something unpleasant happens at the beginning or middle of the story. You know that it's all going to end well so you are able to sit back and simply enjoy the movie. Life is not that different – by living in the end you can avoid most of the turmoil and trauma you would experience when things aren't going your way.

Life is 10% what happens to you and 90% how you react to it.

- Charles R. Swindoll

By reacting positively to every situation, you can extract the blessing out of it. The seed of opportunity is hidden inside every failure. Don't be the person who sees the glass half empty – be the person who sees the rose while ignoring the thorns.

Each hurdle you encounter on the road to success can help you elevate your game if you choose to focus on the opportunity it contains instead of complaining about the trouble it is causing. Your attitude and mindset are the greatest assets you can ever have. Without the right mindset, you can't become successful at anything. The mindset of success is all about turning even the most disheartening failure into a massive opportunity for growth.

When things aren't going your way, remember this: "Every time I thought I was being rejected from something good, I was actually being re-directed to something better" (Maraboli, 2013).

This really is the truth. While things may not make sense right now, the dots always do connect in hindsight. Every day you are getting closer to your goal. Don't stop believing in yourself and your dreams.

Even the incidents that seem to disorient you and throw you off track are there to prepare you for the ultimate success you are going to experience. You need to persevere and keep your sight fixed on your goals. Live each day as if you have already achieved everything you ever wanted to achieve. One day, it will happen!

Fear – More Friend Than Foe

Chapter Summary

- Everyone experiences fear – there are no exceptions to this rule. The only difference is in the way we deal with fear. Those who choose a mediocre life see fear as something bad that must be kept away at all times. Successful people see fear as an indicator of what they really need to do. It's often the things that we fear doing the most that carry the greatest capacity for growth.

- More often than not, the consequences are never as bad as we imagine them to be. The cost of not taking action is always very high. Instead of focusing on what you fear, think about what you are missing by not doing the things that you fear most?

- Failing at something is not the worst thing that can happen to you. The worst thing you can do to yourself is to accept any temporary setback as a permanent failure. Failure is final only if you give up and decide to not try again.

- Every time you encounter a failure, just know that you are developing greater mental toughness. In the same way that you lift heavier weights to become stronger, you have to take on new challenges in life to become a stronger and more successful person.

- Self-awareness is the most important key to success. Successful people exercise control over their mind and emotions instead of being controlled by them. You need to constantly remain aware of the type of thoughts and emotions you are experiencing.

- Write down your negative self-talk then create a positive counter-statement for each one. Once you have the positive statements, burn the negative self-talk.

- Gratitude is the most powerful form of prayer. Any situation can be transformed from a negative to a positive one through the power of gratitude.

- Every time you find yourself getting worried about something that may happen in the future, pause for a moment and think about the opposite coming true. Heaven and hell are within your mind. You can create a living hell for yourself by constantly dwelling on the negative or you can experience the serenity of heaven by focusing on that which is pleasant and uplifting.

- Every day you are getting closer to your goal. Don't stop believing in yourself and your dreams. Even the incidents that seem to disorient you and throw you off track prepare you for the ultimate success you are going to experience.

Chapter Four: Courage – Staying True to Yourself and Your Values

Success is not final, failure is not fatal: it is the courage to continue that counts.

- Winston S. Churchill

Maya Angelou famously said, "Courage is the most important of all the virtues because, without courage, you can't practice any other virtue consistently." I can't emphasize how true this is. Courage truly is the mother of all virtues. You can't practice honesty without courage. Nor can you persevere without courage.

Practicing all other virtues requires mastering the art of staying courageous at all times. This doesn't mean it is easy. If it was easy, anyone would do it. Everyone has the potential to be courageous but very few people practice it.

Courage – Staying True to Yourself and Your Values

To be courageous, you need to know yourself and your values. Martin Luther King, Jr. said, "If a man has not discovered something that he will die for, he isn't fit to live." When you know what's really important to you, you'll stay faithful to it no matter how many trials and tribulations you are subjected to.

Knowing and understanding your why is critical. Your why has to be something that appeals to you at a deep emotional level. For instance, a mother would do anything in the world to protect her child if she felt her child's life was in danger in any way. Her passion for protecting her child trumps any fear she may have about getting harmed in the process.

You need to have passion and hunger for your goals. Only then will you act with courage no matter how huge the challenge in front of you is.

The Courage To Say No

It takes discipline, courage, wisdom, and great strength to say no to everything that's not right for you. It's easy to say yes and allow yourself to be swayed in different directions. Most people settle for a life of mediocrity because they choose the path of least resistance. Greatness requires you to swim against the tide – to do things that no one else would do.

Can you say no to a night of partying when you must stay home to complete the project you are working on? Do you have the ability to say no to the drink you shouldn't be having because of the effect alcohol has on your body and mind? Do you have it in you to walk away from everything that's not right for you and choose only that which serves your long-term good?

Most people can't do it. They live their lives jumping from one distraction to another. They choose what feels good in the moment instead of what is really good for them.

Saying no often means walking alone as you are choosing something that others are not. It's not an easy road and it's often quite lonely. You have to want success more badly than you want to breathe – that's when you'll find the courage and the strength to say no.

You may lose many people along the way as they won't understand your decisions. They will feel threatened by the fact that you are choosing to do something different. Are you willing to stand up for your choices and your convictions even if it means losing some important relationships on the road to success?

Keep your eyes fixed on the future you are building for yourself – it takes hard work, persistence, and sacrifices. The clearer your vision

Courage – Staying True to Yourself and Your Values

is, the stronger your resolve to say no would be to everything that can distract you from your path.

Discipline yourself to not fall for temptations when everyone else around you lacks your standards and vision. Say no to that slice of pizza that you know very well would crush your fitness routine. Say no to alcohol when you know you have to wake up the next morning to be at the gym. Never allow your standards to slip just because your peers don't hold themselves up to those same standards.

Success is not a lottery that you win with a single stroke of luck. It is the cumulative result of your consistent actions. How frequently you say no to everything that's wrong for you and yes to all that's good for you contributes to your success. Every single day counts. Champions don't have off days. That one day when you snoozed the alarm and went back to sleep could set you back by a year or two or more.

You have to say no to everything that is tempting, easy, and feels good in the moment. You can't achieve anything worthwhile without saying yes to doing the most difficult and challenging things that would eventually reward you with a magnificent life.

No one likes getting out of a warm bed when it is freezing cold outside but that's what winners do because the success that they want is more important to them than a few more hours of sleep. Besides, the sleep you get once the alarm has gone off is going to be guilt-ridden. You won't wake up feeling good about yourself. You'll feel like a failure. You failed at the very first task you had set for yourself – waking up on time.

On the other hand, if you can find the courage and the strength to get out of bed and do what you must do, then your self-confidence will increase. By accomplishing your first goal, you are setting up a positive precedent for the rest of your day. Your self-esteem is on a high and you know you can accomplish anything that you set your mind to.

Each no that you say works like compound interest. Eventually, you'll get your payment and what you will receive will be far greater than just a monetary reward. Money will come to you instead of you having to chase after it. More importantly, you will enjoy a higher quality of life with great health, wonderful relationships, high self-respect, and real freedom.

Saying no could also mean opting out of relationships that aren't good for your mental and emotional health. It could mean walking out of a dysfunctional marriage or distancing yourself from a toxic family member. That's not going to be easy, especially when the other person doesn't want to let you go. Do you have it in yourself to do this?

Courage – Staying True to Yourself and Your Values

By saying no to the wrong relationships, you will make room for better new relationships to find you. If you remain stuck in a toxic and dysfunctional relationship, you'll never get to experience the joy of being truly connected to another human being. Christopher Columbus is attributed to having said, "You can never cross the ocean unless you have the courage to lose sight of the shore."

Saying no requires you to move out of your comfort zone. You have to do something that's uncomfortable and likely even uncomfortable to you.

What Do You Say NO to?

X No to everything that takes you away from your goals

X No to all that's not aligned with your values and vision

X No to all your bad and self-destructive habits

X No to negative and toxic people

X No to complaining and feeling sorry for yourself

X No to yielding and giving up

X No to trying to fit in

✗ No to all the comfort zones you have built for yourself

✗ No to all attempts at cutting corners

✗ No to chasing the next shiny object that can't provide you with true fulfillment

What Do You Say YES to?

✓ Yes to anything and everything that makes you stronger

✓ Yes to doing the right thing when it's very hard, *especially* when it's very hard

✓ Yes to temporary pain and suffering that takes you closer to your goals

✓ Yes to hard work

✓ Yes to personal integrity

✓ Yes to your future

✓ Yes to walking alone when no one else shares or understands your goals and vision

✓ Yes to living every moment of your life with authenticity, purpose, and intention

Courage – Staying True to Yourself and Your Values

✓ Yes to pushing yourself to your limits

✓ Yes to getting up and coming back stronger every time you get knocked down

The Courage to Hold Yourself Accountable

We all make mistakes – some are small while others are big. Mistakes are inevitable and in many ways essential. The most successful people make more mistakes than anyone else. What sets them apart from the rest of the human race is their ability to take responsibility and hold themselves accountable.

When things go wrong, the successful among us don't look for someone to put the blame on. They ask themselves where they went wrong, and, more importantly, what they can do about it now. Feeling guilty is not an option because guilt prevents us from taking full responsibility. It leaves us feeling sorry for ourselves without having to really do anything about the situation.

All of us have done things we know we shouldn't do. We've let others down, and, much worse, we have let ourselves down. Disappointment is part of the human experience. We are all fundamentally and profoundly flawed. The only thing that distinguishes successful people from the rest is the fact that they never blame others

– they hold themselves accountable because the only person whose actions they can control is their own.

Taking responsibility means accepting that you are responsible for everything that is happening to you in your life right now. That doesn't imply you have caused or created the problems you are facing. It does mean you take full responsibility to solve these problems and challenges. You know that you are the only one who has the power to change your life. When you spend precious energy blaming others, you are prolonging your suffering because you can't change anyone except yourself.

Most people give up very easily. One critical comment from someone can ruin their entire day. They allow one challenging day to turn into a week of failure. They let one setback become the story of their entire life.

Successful people acknowledge their mistakes – they take ownership of every single thing that's happening in their life. They look for solutions instead of getting sucked into a spiral of negativity and hopelessness. They understand that life is full of ups and downs. Sometimes things go right – other times they don't. No matter what the circumstances are like, there is always a chance to learn and grow.

Courage – Staying True to Yourself and Your Values

Winners understand that even when they aren't getting what they had been aiming for, they are still acquiring an education. This education is the most priceless thing they can have because it provides them with the skills and mindset to rebuild anything.

They understand that setbacks and failures are simply small chapters, different seasons, in their life. No matter how things are looking in the moment, they never stop believing in themselves or their dreams.

Winners are a minority – but they are the ones who change the world. It is these people who have defined the course of human history because they are not talkers – they are doers. These people don't look for the easy way out by pointing fingers at others. They do the hard thing in every situation – by going inward and looking at their own flaws. Not in a self-loathing or self-annihilating way but in a practical way so that they can work on their flaws and become better.

Are you ready to become such a person? Do you have it in you to take full responsibility for your entire life? Can you give up finger-pointing and blaming others at once for good?

Greatness can never be achieved without holding oneself accountable. When you hold yourself accountable, you are constantly working on your shortcomings. This compels you to raise the bar even higher for yourself. And that's the key to success.

How successful you are going to become in life depends entirely upon the person that you are and the person that you are willing to become. Only an extraordinary person can live an extraordinary life. Greatness is not something elusive that only a few people are born with. Each one of us has the potential for it. The only difference lies in the fact that some people realize it while others don't.

I want to urge you to hold yourself accountable from now on. When you say you are going to do something, whether you say it to yourself or to others – do it! Take your word and your commitments seriously. When things don't go your way, don't look for someone else to put the blame on. Instead, go inwards and analyze what you could have done better and then do things better the next time.

I want you to become extremely resilient. Don't sit around and moan over your mistakes. Learn from them quickly and move on to your next goal. Never accept any failure as the end of your story. Live in the consciousness of all your goals having already been realized and accept everything that is happening right now as the plot of the story that is leading you to the realization of your ultimate goals.

The Courage to be Disliked

Courage – Staying True to Yourself and Your Values

No matter how nice and wonderful you are, there will always be people who dislike you. The more successful and popular you get, the more haters you'll have. That's just life!

Most people want to be liked more than they want to be successful. You must understand that the road to success is often a lonely one. Very few people will understand your dreams. You'll have to get comfortable being alone and with being disliked.

The vast majority of people have settled for a life of mediocrity. They are not, however, willing to believe this. They try to convince themselves that they don't have what they want because life has been unfair to them in some way. Every person has the exact same number of hours in a day. The difference lies in how people spend their time. Most people would much rather give up on their dreams than sacrifice their time in front of the TV every day.

When you are hard at work, they will try to pull you down. After all, it is easier to pull someone down than to raise oneself to a higher standard. To be successful, you'll have to break out of this prison called 'what other people think of me.'

It doesn't matter what anyone thinks of you. Anything that distracts you from your goals and your vision is not worth paying attention to. The king of the jungle walks alone while the wolves and sheep walk around in packs and flocks. Mark Twain said, "Whenever you find yourself on the side of the majority, it is time to reform (or pause and reflect)."

Indeed, the masses are almost always moving in the wrong direction. The desire to conform is a disease that keeps you stuck in the muck of mediocrity. I want to dare you to be different! Be bold enough to speak your mind even when you know that no one is going to agree with you but you know it to be the truth in your own heart. Have the courage to do that which you know is right for you even when no one else would dare do it.

Success is a long and lonely road. Not everyone can walk on it nor can everyone make it till the end. If you are still reading this book, then I want to tell you that you are amongst the minority who have the ability to make it to the end.

Never dim your own sparkle just to fit in with all those who have chosen a dull and mediocre existence. It is better to be alone than in the company of people who bring you down. At the same time, you must understand that the greatest skill you can ever master is the art of emotional control.

Don't allow yourself to get emotionally fettered by the negative comments of other people. People who have the time and energy to

Courage – Staying True to Yourself and Your Values

hate on others are always unhappy with their own lives. Have you ever come across a happy and successful person who goes around hating on others or judging those who are less successful than they are? I haven't come across anyone like that and I am sure you haven't either.

Bless your haters because they are really hurting inside. They want to be better – they want more. They lack the courage and the determination to realize their dreams. When they come across someone who has what they would like to have for themselves, they find it easiest to hate on them. Winners do things differently – when they come across someone who has what they would like to have, they want to find out exactly how they got there. They are so busy learning from others that they have no time to hate on anyone.

A person who lives their life based on the opinions of others can never achieve true greatness because, at the end of the day, each of us is answerable to our own self. We have all come into this world for a specific purpose – a very unique soul agenda. If we are too afraid to embrace our purpose and our path for fear of what other people would think, then we are never going to attain greatness.

The world would have never received some of its greatest artistic masterpieces if Monet had left painting when his works were heavily criticized by both art critics and the public alike. At the time, most people felt that his paintings were downright ugly, lacking in form, and looked unfinished. Now, his works are studied in the finest art colleges in the world. Art collectors spend millions of dollars buying original Monet paintings. What would have happened if Monet had given up painting when he received the first round of criticism from professional art critics? (McNee, 2021).

Obviously, Monet believed more in himself than in his critics. I want to urge you to turn a deaf ear to all the criticism. If there is something constructive on offer, then by all means, you should take it into account. When someone is spewing pure vitriol, you need to understand that they are fighting a battle within themselves. What they are saying has very little to do with you and has everything to do with them.

History is full of countless stories of great men and women who chose to follow their hearts and do what they felt they were here to do, even when the entire world criticized them. If you want to be successful, then you must have the courage to stand alone for what you believe in even if the entire world was against it.

Use the hate and dislike you receive as fuel to become an even better version of yourself. In Arnold Schwarzenegger's words, "Always think of yourself as special. And think, 'I'm going to prove to myself and the rest of the world that I can do it" (Bornstein, 2021).

Courage – Staying True to Yourself and Your Values

Always strive to be different. Being 'normal' will get you an average and mediocre life. Being different requires strength and courage.

They laugh at me because I'm different; I laugh at them because they're all the same.

- Kurt Cobain

The Importance of Integrity - You're Only Cheating Yourself in the End

Most people want to claim the prize without ever finding the persistence to earn it. They say they want to live an extraordinary life but they never make more than an average effort at anything. They proclaim wanting to be rich while never doing anything to change their ordinary and poverty-minded habits.

If you have stuck with me this far, you obviously aren't one of these people. You are amongst a rare breed of humanity that's constantly hungry for more. You do the things that everyone else says are too hard. You despise mediocrity and crave excellence in every area of life.

Excellence can never exist without integrity. The student who cheated in the exam to get his degree may still get his degree but he'll never acquire the knowledge and the wisdom of the student who burns the midnight oil to understand his subject. The athlete who cheated to win a gold medal may receive accolades and praise from others but he loses respect in his own eyes.

Integrity is what you are doing even when no one is watching you. It's the ability to do the right thing under all circumstances despite the consequences. Integrity means standing up for your values and your beliefs even when no one else is on your side.

Most people would cut corners when no one is watching. They think: What's the harm? No one will ever find out. They have lived their life caring about what other people think of them. They care more about a stranger's opinion of them than they do about their own opinion of themselves.

Even when you think no one is watching you, there is still someone who is watching you every single moment of the day. That person is YOU. Even when you are completely alone, your self-respect, your honor, and your pride are watching you. When you compromise your integrity, you are bringing down your self-respect, honor, and pride.

Acting with integrity enhances your self-esteem and pride. You become an honorable and noble person in your own eyes. It doesn't

Courage – Staying True to Yourself and Your Values

matter what anyone else thinks of you. You are not hungry for anyone's approval. You know who you are and that's enough.

It's easy to cut corners – to cheat a little – to do less than what's needed. Maybe no one will ever find out. You can cheat the entire world but not yourself. You fail in your own eyes every time you compromise with your integrity, and there's nothing worse than that.

You must develop the habit of doing the right thing consistently – whether anyone is looking or not. Be the person who does things and not the one who talks about doing them. So don't just say you will do this or that. Let your results speak for themselves.

Most people chase money for the sake of it. Money without morals is a recipe for disaster. The most successful people don't run after money – they are obsessed with their vision. They love what they do – money just happens to be how they keep scores in the game. It's not the success that matters so much but the growth that you experience to become successful. It is your greatest asset because you can never lose it. It's yours forever. Even if you lost everything, you can rebuild it because you have developed the skills and mindset to do so.

Living with integrity doesn't mean doing the right thing when it is convenient. It means doing the right thing every single day, every moment of your life. There are no off days. You can't bend your morals and your values to suit the circumstances. You stick to doing what is right regardless of the consequences and in spite of what is convenient.

The person whose respect you need the most is you. Hence, never let yourself down. Don't allow yourself to slip when no one is looking. It takes hard work, patience, and a lot of personal sacrifices to create anything of value in life. Most people like things easy. They want to sit on the couch and eat pizza while dreaming of a great body. They want to enjoy luxury vacations without having to do the hard work to attain that level of success and financial independence from which such things would become affordable and easy to enjoy.

Always be the person who wants only what they have worked for – because that's when you can truly enjoy the rewards. Otherwise, even your pleasure would be guilt-ridden. Self-loathing would mar any true enjoyment you may derive.

Fall in love with the grind and not the reward – that's what integrity is about. When you stop being dazzled by the rewards, the rewards begin to chase you. You get to enjoy the best things that life has to offer but you aren't a slave to them.

Don't cheat – don't take the easy path – don't cut corners – don't try to make things easy – don't lower your standards. Integrity means maintaining your standards even when no one is looking. It means

Courage – Staying True to Yourself and Your Values

standing up for that which you believe in even when no one else is by your side. It means being the highest and best version of yourself every single day of life – whether anyone else notices it or not. Integrity means valuing your self-respect more than your desire for praise or reward from others. It means having the courage to walk alone when there's no one else to support you. It means being your own best friend, your own greatest critic, and your own biggest fan at all times.

An extraordinary life is built on extraordinary integrity. Are you ready to live with the highest level of integrity and create a life that others can only dream of?

Chapter Summary

- Courage truly is the mother of all virtues.

- To be courageous, you need to know yourself and your values. When you know what's really important to you, you'll stay faithful to it no matter how many trials and tribulations you are subjected to.

- Most people settle for a life of mediocrity because they choose the path of least resistance. Greatness requires you to swim against the tide – to do things that no one else would.

- Saying no often means walking alone as you are choosing something that others are not. It's not an easy road and it's often quite lonely. You have to want success more than you want to breathe – that's when you'll find the courage and the strength to say no.

Courage – Staying True to Yourself and Your Values

- Discipline yourself to not fall for temptations when everyone else around you lacks your standards and vision.

- The most successful people make more mistakes than anyone else. What sets them apart from the rest of the human race is their ability to take responsibility and hold themselves accountable.

- Most people give up very easily. One critical comment from someone can ruin their entire day. They allow one challenging day to turn into a week of failure. They let one setback become the story of their entire life.

- Successful people acknowledge their mistakes – they take ownership of every single thing that's happening in their life. They look for solutions instead of getting sucked into a spiral of negativity and hopelessness.

- Most people want to be liked more than they want to be successful. You must understand that the road to success is often a lonely one. Very few people will understand your dreams. You'll have to get comfortable being alone and also with being disliked.

- It doesn't matter what anyone thinks of you. Anything that distracts you from your goals and your vision is not worth paying attention to.

- A person who lives their life based on the opinions of others can never achieve true greatness because each of us is answerable to our own self.

- Always strive to be different. Being 'normal' will get you an average and mediocre life.

- Excellence can never exist without integrity.

- Integrity is what you are doing even when no one is watching you. It's the ability to do the right thing under all circumstances despite the consequences. Integrity means standing up for your values and your beliefs even when no one else is on your side.

- It's easy to cut corners – to cheat a little – to do less than what's needed. Maybe no one will ever find out. You can cheat the entire world but not yourself. You fail in your own eyes every time you compromise your integrity, and there's nothing worse than that.

- Fall in love with the grind and not the reward – that's what integrity is about. When you stop being dazzled by the rewards, the rewards begin to chase you.

Chapter Five: Unshakable Self-Confidence

One important key to success is self-confidence. An important key to self-confidence is preparation.

- Arthur Ashe

Confidence is not something you are born with – it is something you build with experience and accomplishment. The more you experience and accomplish, the more confident you become. This is why having a clearly defined daily routine is essential for long-term success. Having a routine ensures that you are taking consistent action towards realizing your goals.

You are preparing every day to play the big game when the time comes. It could be an important test, a business deal, a fitness competition, or anything else that's important to you. You can't become successful without being well-prepared. When you are well-prepared, you are confident in what you are doing. Even if you don't accomplish your goals immediately, you know you are putting your best foot forward. You don't get disheartened by the setbacks you encounter along the road to success because with each setback, you are acquiring more experience. This experience makes you more confident and helps you elevate your game to the next level.

Also, when you have an established routine that you stick to for better or for worse, you are always moving in the direction of your goals. You do what needs to be done irrespective of how you are feeling. Of course, some days, you just don't want to do the work – you feel tired, angry, frustrated; still, you do what needs to be done. Consistently doing what needs to be done despite the emotional highs and lows you may experience is what truly builds self-confidence.

Being self-confident also means believing in yourself even when no one else believes in you. You don't care about the approval or opinion of others because you already know who you are and what you are capable of. You don't get thrown off track just because someone said a harsh word or criticized how you do things. Everyone is entitled to have an opinion. There's no need for it to affect you, especially when it doesn't serve your efforts in realizing your goals or in becoming the highest and best version of yourself.

Be the Most Confident Person in the Room

Unshakable Self-Confidence

There is nothing more attractive than confidence. I'm not talking about being cocky or braggadocious. A truly self-confident person is self-assured. They don't try to deliberately attract attention to themselves – they also don't deflect attention away from themselves. They are comfortable being in the spotlight when it's for good reason. They also don't hungrily hanker to be in that spotlight. They already believe in themselves; other people's approval and attention aren't that important to them.

Confidence is something that's very hard to fake. From that perspective, the old fake it till you make it mantra can work only so much when you want to be the most confident person in the room. I'm not saying that you would read this chapter and tomorrow you'll be the most confident person in the room. Building confidence requires time, patience, and hard work. It is built by doing difficult things on a regular basis. After all, to achieve anything extraordinary in life you need to put in an extraordinary amount of effort and hard work.

Being confident doesn't mean that you are going to walk into the room thinking there's no one better than you. It means being self-assured enough to know that you don't have to compare yourself with anyone. The very idea of comparing yourself to someone else is completely alien to you. You are not competing with anyone else. You don't have to prove yourself to anyone.

Real confidence is about knowing that you are neither above another person nor are you below them. You are just you – a unique, incredible human being. There has never been anyone like you, never will be, in this world at any other point in time. The only competition you have is your own self. You strive to be the better-than-the-best version of yourself every day. The only person you compare yourself with is who you were yesterday.

Straighten Up - Look Like the Most Confident Person

If I ask you to think about the most confident person you have met in your life, what do they look like? How do they carry themselves? Do they keep their shoulders back and their spine straight or do they hunch over?

I am going to let you in on a big secret. If you want to immediately look more confident, all you have to do is stand up or sit up tall and straight. Keep your chin parallel to the floor and look others in the eye when you are talking to them.

Simply owning your space by keeping your body upright has a miraculous effect on our confidence levels. You immediately feel stronger, more powerful and imposing than you would ever feel with a slumped body.

In the Marines, this is one of the first things that new recruits are taught. We are expected to hold ourselves to the highest standards possible and that begins with carrying our bodies with dignity, pride, and the right posture.

How we hold our bodies sends out a strong message to others. It tells them what we think about ourselves – whether we believe in ourselves or not. Can you even imagine what it would look like if you saw a soldier slouching in a military parade?

The biggest reason why you want to maintain excellent posture at all times is because of the way it makes you feel – strong, proud, and confident!

Your Ego is Your Greatest Enemy – Distinguishing Between Confidence and Cockiness

The most successful and self-confident people don't feel any need to prove themselves to others. They are the silent winners and the humble champions. They don't do things to be glorified by others. Their commitment is to their purpose, integrity, and values. They know that the greatest reward in life is maximum self-growth and the fulfillment that comes from consistently becoming a better-than-the-best version of oneself.

Winners are never satisfied – every time they climb a mountain, they start looking for a new one to climb. Of course, they celebrate their achievements but they don't sit around and boast about it. Growth is what they are truly after – all the rewards and glory they receive is simply a byproduct of their passion for self-improvement.

The biggest difference between a confident person and an over-confident or cocky person is that the former never think that they have learned everything there is to learn. They think of themselves as beginners no matter how far ahead in the game they are. They have an insatiable desire to learn and become better. The latter, on the other hand, think that they are better than everyone else. They know everything there is to know. Such a person can never grow beyond a certain point. Their growth becomes stunted and they remain stuck in the past.

Confident people possess what in Zen Buddhism is called the 'beginner's mind' – they are always open to new knowledge. They aren't afraid to re-evaluate their methods and mechanisms. They are also not afraid to admit it when they are wrong. Egoistic people cling to their beliefs even when those ideas aren't serving them anymore. Their ego prevents them from reaching their highest potential. They are more interested in being liked and glorified by others than they are in their own growth.

Unshakable Self-Confidence

A confident person is never threatened by another person who is good at what they are doing. They admire other successful people and strive to learn from them. Egoistic people try to pull others down. Small-minded people live from a place of scarcity. They feel they need to cut other people down to make themselves appear taller.

The ego is also the enemy of self-improvement as it prevents you from recognizing your own faults. You can never attain long-term success without the desire to consistently keep evaluating your flaws and working on them. The potential for growth and improvement is infinite. You can't allow yourself to become smug at any point because there is always the next level of accomplishment and success that you can attain.

Egoistic people also have this idea that certain tasks are beneath them. Self-confident people never think of any task as too small or menial. They understand that every task is respectable. They're willing to get down and dirty, especially when they are starting out with something new and have no choice but to do many things all by themselves.

Never let the voice of your ego obfuscate your judgment. Take a stand for your values and devote yourself fully to the pursuit of your goals, but never for the sake of receiving glory from others. The ego loves flattery – it is often blinded by the desire to be liked, approved, and appreciated by others. Don't let your ego rule you. Who you are in your eyes is all that matters. The only person you are truly answerable to is the one you face in the mirror every day.

Shun your ego and embrace your true self. Hunger for money and fame can lead you only so far. The people who truly change the world and leave a legacy behind are the ones who are driven by something much deeper than that. They carry a vision for a better, more beautiful world in which everyone's lives are improved. True satisfaction doesn't come from the ego's glorification – it comes from knowing you're really doing what you have come here to do.

The ego really is your enemy. It can distract you from your path and compel you to run after that which will never give you any true fulfillment. By learning to keep your ego quiet, you can begin to truly hear the voice of your intuition. It really doesn't matter whether someone else likes you or not – keeping your self-respect intact is the only thing you should strive for.

The Power of Conviction – Why it's Important to Believe in Yourself

Your mind is the most powerful tool at your disposal. Whatever you believe to be true at the deepest level of your subconscious becomes your reality.

Unshakable Self-Confidence

Imagine if you lost your memory completely and everyone around you told you that you are a marine, how do you think you would conduct yourself? Would you conduct yourself differently if you were told instead that you are a primary school teacher?

Your mental concept of who you are defines how you conduct yourself in this world. If you want to become one of the best in your field, you have to start out by believing you are outstanding and extraordinary.

Once you start believing in your own power and greatness, everything about you changes. You carry your body differently – your tone, your posture, the way you make eye contact – everything changes for the better.

No matter where you are in life right now, you can change everything for the better by simply believing in yourself and your potential.

The next time you find yourself making an effort that is less than what you are truly capable of, ask yourself, "What's on my mind?" or, "What am I thinking about?" Most likely, you'll find yourself thinking about the obligation instead of the opportunity that is in front of you.

This is the difference between great people and those who live ordinary lives. The latter do the minimum to get by – the former, on the other hand, go overboard. They think differently – they see things differently. It's not the short-term reward they are after but long-term growth and success.

Believing in yourself means holding on to the highest possible version of yourself every single day. This means you are always focusing on the opportunities that are in front of you – even when things appear to be grim and hopeless. Always remember that character is built in the darkest hours of our lives. You become strong by doing difficult things that stretch your endurance and fortitude to its limits.

To be great, you have to consistently keep breaking your own records. Conviction is about believing that no matter how great you are right now, you can always become better. It's about finding pleasure and gratification in the process of becoming the better-than-the-best version of yourself.

When you truly believe in yourself, you are always looking for opportunities. You wake up every day roaring to yourself, "I AM ALIVE!" You don't do things because that's what's expected of you or because someone else wants you to do something. You do them because you see the opportunity to become your best self.

Unshakable Self-Confidence

If you want to achieve something you have never achieved before, then you have to do the things that you have never done before. It all starts with changing your mindset.

The next time you have to do something and you must do something, think of it as an opportunity. Even if you can't see exactly how it's helping you, I can guarantee you that every challenge you are facing right now is taking you closer to your ultimate goal. Be excited about facing these challenges. Remain obsessed with your goal and you will find the strength to overcome any adversity.

Self-worth is built by doing things that are worthy – the hard things that test your limits. Every single human being has infinite potential but very few tap into it because that requires subjecting oneself to stressors – things that are painful at first.

You have to push yourself into a state where adaptation becomes your one and only choice. You either do or die. When your body and mind are desperate to survive, they will take you to the highest level of your potential.

You have to get out of the mindset of what you can get away with and instead focus on finding out what you are truly capable of. You must become completely obsessed with pushing yourself to your limits.

As soon as you get to one breaking point, you push yourself to the next one. This is how you build a strong body and an indestructible mind!

For that, you have to truly believe that you are capable of greatness. There is a giant inside you just waiting to come out. You can bring this giant out only by falling in love with hard work – with the daily grind that most people would much rather make excuses for.

Practice Humility Everyday

It doesn't matter how rich, successful or knowledgeable you are, there's always room for becoming better. Truly successful people understand that they can never know and understand everything. Every time they crack a puzzle, there is always a new, more difficult and challenging one to be solved.

Simplicity is a form of humility, and simplicity is a sign of true greatness. Meekness is a sign of humility, and meekness is a sign of true strength.

– Vince Lombardi

Successful people are constantly learning and growing. They don't have an ego so they like to learn from everyone – even from the very young or inexperienced. They know that sometimes the greatest ideas and insights can come from the most unlikely sources.

Unshakable Self-Confidence

We can't change anything without first accepting what is. You won't be able to go where you want to be if you can't accept the truth of where you currently are in life. It takes humility to know and accept your weaknesses. It takes humility to admit it when you're wrong. It takes humility to admit that you don't have all the answers and solutions. When you're humble, you can learn from others who may know many things better than you do.

Being close-minded and egoistic is the greatest disease in life. I'm not saying that you shouldn't be proud of yourself. You should definitely believe in your own greatness because what you believe eventually becomes your experience.

I'm just reminding you that the line between pride and arrogance is a thin one. Believe in yourself but always strive to become better. It is easier to be humble when the only person you care about impressing is your own self. You aren't competing to prove yourself as better than anyone else. You are your own competition and the only person you want to be better than is who you were yesterday.

A humble person is constantly asking "What am I truly capable of?" Every time they achieve something, they ask themselves: What more am I capable of? They are always pushing themselves harder – breaking through their limitations and boundaries. They always want to bear more pressure and do more. Becoming smug is never an option to them. As long as they are alive and breathing, there is potential to grow even further by moving beyond their comfort zone.

Believe not only in who you are but also in who you can become. That vision has to be compelling enough to want you to push yourself harder every day. For that, you have to keep your feet grounded – be realistic about where you are in the moment and what you need to do to get where you want to be.

Humility means standing naked with your inadequacies and having the courage to admit that you are not perfect. You neither allow your ego to get inflated with praise nor do you let yourself get wounded by criticism. It really doesn't matter what anyone else thinks about you. All that matters is what you think about yourself when you are completely by yourself. The only person who is always going to be with you is you yourself. That's the one person whose respect you must have at all times.

Don't ever settle for less than what you are capable of and who you can be. Be grateful for all that you are blessed with and for everyone who has helped you. Gratitude and humility go hand-in-hand. Without humility, you can't be grateful and without gratitude, you can't be truly humble. Gratitude multiplies your blessings – whatever you are grateful for, you receive more of.

Stay humble, stay grateful, and remain blessed!

Start Off with Small Wins

Self-confidence is critical for success. Is it something you can build?

Here's a quote from Barrie Davenport that sums up the answer to this question perfectly: *Self-confidence can be learned, practiced, and mastered – just like any other skill. Once you master it, everything in your life will change for the better* (Christian, 2018).

Confidence is a muscle like any other. You build it by taking consistent action. Your success becomes your testimony.

How will you ever know what you are capable of if you don't start doing the work to realize your dreams? You need to begin now – not tomorrow, not the day after. Right now!

Most people keep waiting for the perfect time, perfect day, and perfect set of circumstances. They don't realize that these things are never going to be perfect. Life and everything in it is imperfect. You don't have to do things perfectly to become successful – you need to get started and keep working with perseverance.

If that's too big a goal to start with, then start with small things. Harvard professor Teresa Amabile has proven with research that keeping track of your small wins does wonders for boosting self-confidence and motivation (Amabile & Kramer, 2011).

Every single win – whether big or small – impacts the circuitry of your brain. You build new neural-pathways of success. Every time you achieve something, your brain secretes dopamine that makes you feel good about yourself. When you are consistently receiving a dopamine hit, you feel good about yourself on a regular basis.

In fact, it's not an exaggeration to say that the small wins are even more important than the big ones. Why? Well, because it is the small wins that pave the way to big wins. To achieve any major goal, you have to break down the steps to get there into small digestible chunks which translate into daily, weekly, and monthly actions.

Little by little, every day, you move closer to your goal. When you look at the peak of a mountain, it's hard to imagine how you'll ever get there. When you are focused on taking one step at a time, you eventually manage to get to the top of the mountain. Following this logic, it is each step along the way that you need to turn into your micro goals and celebrate every little accomplishment. You'll also be able to maintain the momentum and keep yourself focused.

I'm going to give you two more very important actions you can do every day to boost your self-confidence. These will be the two small wins you will start each day with.

Never Put Your Alarm Clock on Snooze

Once you have set your alarm clock, consider it set in stone. When the alarm goes off, get up from your bed no matter how tired or lazy you are feeling. Don't say to yourself, "One more minute," or, "Five more minutes."

Once the alarm has gone off, you can't go back to your peaceful sleep, anyway. Even if you do manage to squeeze in a short nap, it would be guilt-ridden. When you finally wake up, you will have lost precious time. Instead of feeling on top of your day, you will feel as if everything is spiraling out of your control.

On the other hand, if you can get yourself to do the hard thing by getting out of bed and springing to action the moment your alarm clock goes off, you have already accomplished your first win for the day.

My mentor told me once, how you start your day is how you'll finish it. When you are starting your day on a note of failure and guilt, that's how you'll end up spending most of your day. On the other hand, doing the tough thing boosts your self-esteem. You feel you can trust yourself – you have more faith in your abilities; you are better prepared to tackle any and all challenges that may come up throughout the course of the day.

Before you go to bed tonight, decide what time you are going to wake up. Set your alarm clock and resolve to wake up at that time no matter what.

I also recommend that you place your alarm clock in another room or at least far away from your bed. This way you'll have to get out of bed to turn it off so you would be compelled to move out of your comfort zone.

Another suggestion I would like to share: buy a real alarm clock instead of using your phone as one. Most people can't resist looking at their phones first thing in the morning. They check their messages, emails, social media, etc., and get totally sucked into the online world. Minutes turn into hours and their day starts on a note of total chaos. Also, you are putting yourself in a reactive mode. You haven't prepared yourself for the day but you are already inundated by the demands placed on you.

If you are still planning to use your phone's alarm clock, I suggest that you use one of those apps that block out access to the phone for a fixed number of hours each day. You can set rules for phone usage so that you won't be accessing your messages, email, social media, etc., between 9 pm to 8 am every day.

Having an app that blocks access to these apps every day during your specified time period is a total game changer. None of us is strong enough to resist the temptations of the online world all the time. Hence, apps like these are extremely helpful. You can exclude any of the apps that you need for your morning routines such as the meditation, exercise, or journaling app that you are using.

Make Your Bed Every Single Morning

In the marines, one of the things we were expected to do every morning was to make our bed with meticulous perfection. Someone very wise once said, "How you do anything is how you do everything."

While making the bed is one small task that takes only a few minutes every day, it sets the tone for how we'll do everything else throughout our day.

In a famous speech given by Naval Adm. William H. McRaven, he said:

> It was a simple task — mundane at best. But every morning we were required to make our bed to perfection. It seemed a little ridiculous at the time,

particularly in light of the fact that we were aspiring to be real warriors, tough battle-hardened SEALs, but the wisdom of this simple act has been proven to me many times over.

If you make your bed every morning you will have accomplished the first task of the day. It will give you a small sense of pride, and it will encourage you to do another task and another and another. By the end of the day, that one task completed will have turned into many tasks completed. Making your bed will also reinforce the fact that little things in life matter. If you can't do the little things right, you will never do the big things right.

And, if by chance you have a miserable day, you will come home to a bed that is made — that you made — and a made bed gives you encouragement that tomorrow will be better.

If you want to change the world, start off by making your bed (McRaven, 2014).

I want to urge you to start your day with two small wins every single day: Get up when your alarm clock goes off and make your bed as soon as you are out of it. This way you won't be tempted to crawl back in and when you finally do get to get on your bed after a day of hard work, it will feel truly rewarding and comforting. You'll fall asleep knowing that you gave your best and did your best – now you deserve to enjoy a good night's sleep.

Living a disciplined life is not easy but discipline is synonymous with success. You can never attain anything worthwhile in life without gaining control over your routine first. How you spend each day of your life defines and determines what you'll achieve in the long run.

Start each day with two small wins. Even if nothing else goes according to plan that day, you still have two wins to fall back on. You got up – you showed up. It's okay that sometimes things don't go the way we would like but tomorrow you'll get another opportunity to begin again. Tomorrow, you'll start again with two small wins!

Chapter Summary

- Confidence is not something you are born with – it is something you build with experience and accomplishment. The more you experience and accomplish, the more confident you become.

- Building confidence requires time, patience, and hard work. It is built by doing difficult things on a regular basis.

- Being confident doesn't mean that you are going to walk into the room thinking there's no one better than you. It means being self-assured enough to know that you don't have to compare yourself with anyone.

Unshakable Self-Confidence

- In the marines, we are expected to hold ourselves to the highest standards possible and that begins with carrying our bodies with dignity, pride, and the right posture.

- A confident person is never threatened by another person who is good at what they are doing. They admire other successful people and strive to learn from them. Egoistic people try to pull others down. Small-minded people live from a place of scarcity. They feel they need to cut other people down to make themselves appear taller.

- Your mind is the most powerful tool at your disposal. Whatever you believe to be true at the deepest level of your subconscious becomes your reality.

- Your mental concept of who you are defines how you conduct yourself in this world. If you want to become one of the best in your field, you have to start out by believing you are outstanding and extraordinary.

- Believing in yourself means holding on to the highest possible version of yourself every single day. Focus on the opportunities that are in front of you – even when things appear to be grim and hopeless. Always remember that character is built in the darkest hours of our lives. You become strong by doing difficult things that stretch your endurance and fortitude to its limits.

- Push yourself into a state wherein adaptation becomes your one and only choice. You either do or die. When your body and mind are desperate to survive, they will take you to the highest level of your potential.

- Humility means standing naked with your inadequacies and having the courage to admit that you are not perfect.

- Confidence is a muscle like any other. You build it by taking consistent action. Your success becomes your testimony.

- Every single win – whether big or small – impacts the circuitry of your brain. You build new neural-pathways of success. Every time you achieve something, your brain secretes dopamine that makes you feel good about yourself. When you are consistently receiving a dopamine hit, you feel good about yourself.

- If you can get yourself to do the hard thing by getting out of bed and springing to action the moment your alarm clock goes off, you have already accomplished your first win of the day.

- While making the bed is one small task that takes only a few minutes every morning, it sets the tone for how we'll do everything else in our day.

- Living a disciplined life is not easy but discipline is synonymous with success. You can never attain anything worthwhile in life without gaining control over your routine first. How you spend each day of your life defines and determines what you'll achieve in the long run.

Part 2
The Game Plan

Chapter Six: The Amateur Mental Toughness Training Program

Success is nothing more than a few simple disciplines, practiced every day; while failure is simply a few errors in judgment, repeated every day. It is the accumulative weight of our disciplines and our judgments that leads us to either fortune or failure.

- Jim Rohn

In part one we worked on your mindset. Now, it is time to build mental toughness by taking action. In this chapter and in the next two chapters following this one, I will share with you practical step-by-step instructions for developing mental toughness.

I want to urge you to not just read these chapters but to act on them. This book will change your life – provided you are ready to give your 100 percent and do the work.

This chapter is for the beginner who is getting started with developing mental toughness. Even if you think you are quite far ahead in your self-development journey, I strongly advise that you do all the exercises listed in Chapters Six, Seven, and Eight. To get the maximum benefit, do them in the sequence that they are laid out in. The exercises build on each other. Doing them sequentially will help with taking action in an organized manner.

Getting Your Attitude Right - Why People with the Wrong Attitude Fail

Attitude really is everything! Your attitude defines and determines every experience of your life.

Let us start with the basics. What exactly is attitude?

According to *Wikipedia*, "In psychology, attitude is a psychological construct, a mental and emotional entity that inheres in or **characterizes a person**. They are complex and are an **acquired state through experiences**. It is an individual's **predisposed state of mind** regarding a value and it is precipitated through a responsive expression towards oneself, a person, place, thing, or event (the attitude object) which in turn influences the individual's thought and action… Attitude can be **formed from a person's past and present**" (2021).

From this definition, it is quite clear that attitude is something that we acquire through our experiences. A series of bad experiences can leave a person with a bad attitude. For example, a middle-aged woman who went through a few dysfunctional relationships and now believes that all men are cheaters who want to exploit women. Another example is the aspiring athlete who gets really close to hitting the goal but loses every time by a small mark. After a while, he started believing that when he gets close to success, he'll always miss the mark at the last minute.

When you are approaching anything new with an attitude acquired from your past negative experience, you are pretty much setting yourself up for failure. How can you succeed at something when you have already failed at it in your mind?

The reason why people with a negative attitude fail consistently is that they are always expecting to fail. They believe that nothing good can ever happen to them. It's only a matter of time before their negative anticipation turns into a self-fulfilling prophecy.

If you want to succeed at anything in life, you have to start out by believing that you have already succeeded. This is where visualization plays a very important role. In your mind's eye, you have to see yourself succeeding and you must believe that you have already succeeded. We will discuss visualization in greater detail in the next section.

Your faith really does determine your fate. You must have faith in yourself and in your ability to succeed. Do not let past disappointments and failures define your current experience of life. No matter what has happened in the past, you can turn things around.

You can succeed at anything you set your mind to. You just have to believe that it's possible and you have to persevere until your positive expectation becomes your joyful reality.

Exercise

Think of an immediate goal you want to achieve (it doesn't matter whether it's a big or a small goal). Now, imagine yourself doing the actions that are necessary for achieving that goal. *How are you feeling? What are your thoughts?*

Write down all your observations on a piece of paper.

Once you have finished writing down all your feelings around that goal, pick out all the negative ideas. Take another piece of paper and write down the opposite of those negative thoughts and feelings.

Again, visualize taking action on your goals. This time when the negative thoughts and feelings begin to surface, take the other piece of paper and read out aloud your new beliefs. You can also read them silently in your mind but there's something really powerful about using your voice to affirm a new belief to yourself.

Repeat this attitude assessment and rectification test for all your goals.

Visualization and Goal Setting - Understand What it is You Want to Achieve

To achieve anything in life, you have to first understand exactly what it is that you want to accomplish. Your goals should inspire and scare you. The legendary motivational speaker, Bob Proctor, says, "Set a goal to achieve something that is so big, so exhilarating that it excites you and scares you at the same time. If you do not get the chills when you set your goal you're not setting big enough goals."

Most people set goals that don't inspire them. Hence, they aren't able to find the motivation to work towards them. Tony Robbins explains this perfectly:

> Many times, people tell me things like, "Well Tony, you are successful in your life because after all, you're so motivated. I'm just lazy." I just tell people you're not lazy, you have impotent goals. What we wanna do is get some goals that will drive you. Some

goals that've got some power behind them. And the way to do that is to realize that right now you are about to create a real future, you're not writing down words on a page (2017).

If your goals don't excite you and scare you, then they aren't good enough to be pursued. You are most likely selling yourself short or as Bob Proctor puts it, "Most people are not going after what they want. Even some of the most serious goal seekers and goal setters, they're going after what they think they can get."

You must raise the bar for yourself. Demand nothing but excellence from yourself. Every time you think about your goals, those thoughts should fill you with thrills and excitement.

Never allow doubts and fears to control you. Instead of wondering how or if you'll ever get there, visualize that you already have everything you are aspiring for. Allow yourself to feel happy and satisfied as if your goals have already been realized. Failure shouldn't be an option. Keep working until you get the final thing you are after.

Any setback that you encounter along the way should further fuel your hunger for success. Train yourself to snap back like a rubber band with double the force after every disappointment.

Know Your Why

To set meaningful goals you have to first know your why. Your why is something that fuels you mentally and emotionally. It's a reason that's so strong and important that you'd stake everything you have and all that you are to get what you are after and to become who you want to be.

Losers think of Plan B. For winners, there is only one plan – there is no choice except that one goal they are laser focused on. It doesn't matter how long it takes or how hard they have to work, they are willing to persevere in the pursuit of their goals.

Exercise

Step One – Define Your Goal

Your goal should be specific and clearly defined. "I want to be rich," is a vague statement. "I want to earn $10,000 a month," is a clear goal.

Be realistic about your goal but don't sell yourself short. If you are earning $2,000 right now and you set the goal as earning $10,000 a month but you don't believe you can actually do it, then that's not a realistic goal. This doesn't mean you should give up on your goal. You need to break down your big goal into small goals. First, set the goal as wanting to earn $2,500 or $3,000 a month or whatever dollar amount feels most realistic to you right now.

Once you get to that goal, raise the bar higher and set the next goal. Raise your goals higher in gradual increments.

Step Two – State Your *Why*

What will you get by achieving your goal and why must you achieve it? One *Why* would be, "I want to earn $10,000 a month so that I can enjoy vacationing at luxury destinations and wearing nice watches."

Another *Why* would be, "I want to earn $10,000 a month so that I can have complete financial independence – I want to have abundant money to do everything I want to do for myself and my family. I want to be free from the drudgery of work I don't want to do so that I can live my life in my own way with full satisfaction."

Which of these *Whys* will really motivate you, especially when the going gets tough and you encounter those times when you just want to quit?

I'm sure if the first one is your *Why*, you'll be tempted to quit as soon as the first few challenges come up. Whereas, with the second one you are after a real transformation – you know that having money would provide you with freedom and the ability to do the things you truly desire to do. You'll get a chance to look after not only your own needs and desires but also those of your loved ones.

Your *Why* can also be completely different from the statement above. The point is it has to be something that's deeply personal to you. It should fire you emotionally every day – enough to get you out of bed and love the grind!

Step Three – Create a Goal Statement

Now that you know your goal and your *why*, it is time to create a goal statement. The language you use for it should be positive and inspiring. A goal statement like, "My goal is to earn $10,000 a month so that I don't have to be someone else's slave," is not a positive or truly inspiring one.

The right statement would be something like, "My goal is to earn $10,000 a month so that I can be financially free and live my best life while helping my loved ones in whatever way I can."

Again, your goal statement is something deeply personal to you. It should provide you with emotional fuel. Be sure to reframe any negative word, phrase, or idea into a positive one to make it truly transformational.

Step Four – Decide on a Timeframe

Without a timeframe, you are bound to get lazy and distracted. You must specify a timeline for achieving your goals. If you don't place any pressure on yourself to achieve your goal by a specific date, you will lose your motivation along the way. You have to feel a sense of urgency to pursue your goal with dedication and single-minded focus.

It's time to add a specific timeframe to your goal statement. Your goal statement would now read something like this: "My goal is to earn $10,000 a month so that I can be financially free and live my best life while helping my loved ones in whatever way I can. I'm achieving this goal by *date-month-year*."

You don't have to know an exact date but give yourself some kind of a deadline and stick to it as much as possible. Another pro tip here: use the language of the present. Instead of saying, "I will achieve," make it, "I am achieving." You want to believe that you have already achieved or you are achieving your goals. There should be no question of tentativeness or probability.

Step Five – Nail Down the *How*

Without an action plan, goals are nothing but wishes. Add to your goal statement exactly how you are going to achieve the goal. Let's say that you are planning to achieve your goal by establishing a successful self-publishing business.

Your goal statement would read: "My goal is to earn $10,000 a month so that I can be financially free and live my best life while helping my loved ones in whatever way I can. I'm achieving this goal by *date-month-year* by running a successful and profitable self-publishing business."

Of course, apart from adding your *how* to your goal statement, you are also going to draft a clear game plan for how you will establish and run a successful business. Be sure to break down the big goal into smaller ones and celebrate each accomplishment along the way.

Step Six – Visualize Your Success

By now you should have a clear picture of exactly what you want to achieve, why you want to achieve it, and how you'll go about it. Form a vision in your mind in which you have already achieved your goal.

Visualize yourself comfortably and happily paying for something you want. See yourself helping others while looking like a successful person dressed in the type of clothes you see yourself wearing as a successful person. Again, your vision will be unique and personal to you. The only criteria is that it should be clear, crisp, and inspiring.

Raise Your Standards - Why You Should Settle for Nothing Less Than Exceptional

An exceptional life begins with exceptional standards. With mediocre standards, you will achieve nothing more than mediocrity. Most people are dreamers – they want all the fancy things that life has to offer but they aren't willing to work for it. They expect to live an exceptional life while having mediocre and average standards for themselves and the type of effort they are willing to put in.

Real satisfaction can never come from following the path of least resistance. It comes from working harder than everyone else and for that, you have to demand more for yourself – you must raise the bar extremely high for what you are willing to accept from yourself. Anything less than exceptional should never be good enough for you. The very words' average, easy, and mediocre shouldn't exist in your vocabulary.

The only difference between successful people and average people is their standards. Successful people hold themselves up to a much higher standard. Average people are busy counting their *shoulds:* I should join the gym; I should work harder at school; I should improve my speech; I should build more skills.

Successful people don't have a list of *shoulds*. They have a list that starts with an action verb: I go to the gym every day; I work hard at school; I am becoming exceptional at my speech and delivery; I continually build more skills to succeed more.

They don't sit around and wait for things to happen. They are always busy making things happen.

The Amateur Mental Toughness Training Program

To raise your standards, metaphorically burn all your boats. As long as you have an exit strategy in mind, you'll never hold yourself up to an exceptionally high standard.

Without raising your standards, you can never create or experience lasting change in your life. Who you are is not a reflection of your desires – it is always a result of your standards.

Our standards are strongly influenced by our environment. If you are always around people who are low energy, then you will yourself become a low energy person. If you spend the vast majority of your time with people who spend most of their time drinking beer and watching football, then that's who you'll become.

To raise your standards, you have to also change who you are spending the vast majority of your time with. The biggest reason why marines are able to perform at extraordinary levels is that we are trained in an extraordinary environment where the bar is raised very high and everyone around has equally high standards for themselves.

Surround yourself with people who aspire for greatness – those who don't just wish for things but who love the daily grind. These are the type of people who wake up before everyone else does. They may not be the best at everything but one thing is for sure – no one can ever outwork them.

Small Habits Equal Big Results - Supporting Habits and Winning Routines to Get You There

Success is not an isolated event that occurs out of the blue. It is the culmination of daily habits supporting your efforts. When you watch a footballer's outstanding performance on the day of the match, what you are witnessing is not a coincidence. It is the climax – the culmination – of hundreds and thousands of hours of training.

While success looks glamorous – the daily grind one has to go through to reach there is far from glamorous. It's painful and repetitive. All successful people understand that success doesn't come without sweat, grit, and suffering. The reason why most people will never become successful is that their primary focus is on being comfortable, avoiding pain and discomfort as much as possible.

These people sacrifice long-term success for short-term comforts. As a result, they suffer in the long term. You only have to think about that person who is addicted to pizza and trash television to know what I am talking about. He may be able to numb himself to the fact that his health is rapidly declining but only for so long. In the long run, the choices he has made will become manifested in the results he'd experience. The price for the faux pleasure of eating junk food in the short run is obesity and having to live with a diseased body in the long term.

Successful people understand that in order to get what they want, they must endure a certain amount of suffering. The more extraordinary the goal, the greater the suffering or sacrifice. They don't want things cheap or easy – they want only the very best in life. In order to have the very best that life can offer, they must become the very best that they can be. Hence, they demand excellence from themselves every single day.

I hated every minute of training, but I said, "Don't quit.

Suffer now and live the rest of your life as a champion."

- Muhammad Ali

Work Harder Than Everyone Else

Most people think that those who are successful simply got lucky. That's far from the truth. From my own observations about the life and habits of successful people, I can tell you that they work harder than everyone else. They may not be the smartest, most talented, or even the cleverest. What they have is extraordinary persistence. They persevere when everyone else quits.

They don't do things to garner praise from others. They do what's right. While others are busy complaining, they are busy finding solutions. When others make excuses for why something can't work out, they are busy making progress to reach the next level.

Set Your Priorities Right

All of us have far too much on our plate than we can possibly handle. The most important habit you can adopt is to set your priorities right.

Which goals are the most important? Which tasks will help you maximize your results? What are the most critical things you must do right now to get closer to your goals?

According to Pareto's Principle, 80 percent of results come from 20 percent of the things that we do. You need to identify this 20 percent that will help maximize your results. Without focused goals, you will end up scattering your energy everywhere.

I would highly recommend reading The 4-Hour Workweek by Timothy Ferriss. This book has a powerful message that you can benefit from, no matter where you are on your road to success. You have to train yourself to spend your time and energy on things that will get you maximum results while you outsource the tasks that are repetitive or require less creativity.

Successful people value their time over money. Money can be earned again but time is a depreciating asset. With every passing minute, you are losing time. You can't bring it back or re-earn it. It is the most limited resource you own. Spend your time wisely to maximize your gains.

Wake Up Early

One habit that most of the world's most successful people have in common is that they wake up early. They don't just attack the day in reactive mode. It's important for them to get themselves centered and grounded to face the day before the rest of the world awakes.

There is something very soothing about the morning air. When you wake up early, you have time to decide how you are going to live that day instead of being attacked by the demands of the day right after you open your eyes. A great resource that I suggest you read is the book The Miracle Morning by Hal Elrod to create some solid daily rituals for yourself.

How you start your day will determine how you spend the rest of it. Start strong and finish strong – that's the mantra I would like you to adopt from now on. Don't go to bed when you are tired – go to bed only when you are done. Don't wake up when you feel like it. Wake up earlier than everyone else because you must!

Invest in Yourself

The greatest investment you can ever make is in your own self. As Brian Tracy puts it, "Your success in life depends more on the person you become than the things you do or acquire" (Silva, 2021).

If you study the lives of highly successful people, you will realize that they are constantly learning and growing. They are usually voracious readers obsessed with personal development.

To become the very best at what you do, you need to constantly keep polishing and advancing your skill sets. The problem with most people is that they acquire a degree or a diploma and think that's what education is about. We live in a world of incessant change and rapid progression. The only type of education that will get you ahead in life is self-education.

You must invest time, energy, and money in taking courses, reading books, participating in masterminds, and hiring coaches. I am not saying that you have to do all this in one go. Depending upon your current financial situation and immediate goals, you can choose some of these options. Always choose the option that will get you maximum results. For instance, reading a book on fat loss can help you develop some powerful insights but you will get faster results if you hire a professional trainer to coach you to get active and lose weight.

Most people don't succeed in business because they try to reinvent the wheel. The fastest way to become successful is to find someone who already has the results that you want and learn from them.

If you want to become massively successful in life, you have to make massive investments in yourself.

Create a Winning Environment - Your Environment is Key to Success or Failure

Jim Rohn famously said, "You are the average of the five people you spend the most time with." Who you keep yourself surrounded by determines how far you will go in life. If you are constantly surrounded by average people who aspire for nothing more than the path of least resistance, then being average is who you will become.

If you are constantly surrounded by broke people, then their incompetent financial habits and poverty mindset will rub off on you as well. As the old adage goes, misery loves company. Indeed, most people like to make excuses for why their life is the way it is. They like to surround themselves with other individuals who are more interested in blaming someone else for their challenges than in taking ownership of their lives and their destiny.

The good news is that greatness also loves company. By surrounding yourself with extraordinary people, you can raise the bar even higher for yourself. As Confucius said, "If you are the smartest person in the room, then you are in the wrong room."

Surround yourself with people who aspire for excellence as well as with those from whom you can learn. You have to find a way to be in the company of individuals who inspire you. In today's times, this is easier than it has ever been in history. All you need to do is download an audiobook or join an online or even an offline coaching program: you'll immediately be in the company of someone you truly admire.

Now, I am not saying that you should abandon all your friends and family who prefer average and mediocre lives. I'm not even saying that there is something wrong with living an average or mediocre life. If you are reading this book and you have made it this far, then you are clearly not one of the masses. You have the soul and the heart of a champion – you crave greatness and excellence. For you, I would say it is important to be intentional with your time.

You can enjoy good times together with family and friends who don't share your passion for excellence but be careful not to adopt their limiting beliefs when you are with them. That's easier said than done! The truth is that we are affected energetically, mentally, emotionally, and physically by the company that we keep.

I strongly advise that you focus on spending the vast majority of your time with people who inspire and uplift you – those who compel you to raise the bar even higher for yourself. The reason why it is easier to perform at extraordinary levels in the marines is that we are all living in an extraordinary environment where excellence is demanded at every step of every day.

Compare that to an environment where the standards for what's expected are lower – like a boy's hostel where everyone smokes, drinks, parties, and stays up late watching television. It would be very hard to keep one's standards high in such an environment.

I am not saying it's impossible because a champion can shine even in the most adverse environment. My point is to illustrate the differences to help you realize that the standards that you have for yourself are in many ways the average of the standards that other people in your environment have for themselves. If you want to take the fastest road to success, then start by changing the company that you keep!

Repetition and Deliberate Learning

What makes champions different from everyone else?

Mindset! Of course!

While everyone else is busy watching Netflix and eating pizza, champions are hard at work mastering their skills. They understand that there are no shortcuts to mastery – it comes with deliberate, intentional repetition, day in and day out.

Another key trait that all champions have in common is a voracious appetite for learning. Champions are always busy figuring out how to take their game to the next level. I'm not just referring to elite athletes but to champions in every area of life.

Learning is not the same as knowing things. Anyone can read a book and boast about knowing a great deal on a subject. You have never truly learned something unless you have made it completely your own.

Think about it – how much information can you retrieve from your memory right now if I asked you to recall everything you studied in high school. I bet there won't be much that you can recall!

If I ask you to recall what you wrote in the report you created last year, you would be more likely to successfully jog your memory. Learning is not about exposing yourself to new information – it's about understanding, interpreting, and internalizing the knowledge.

To live like a champion, repeatedly practice your skills. Even when you gain a great deal of mastery over them, you have to continue aspiring for the next level of greatness. There are no limits to how much you can grow and how far you can go. The only limits are within your own mind. You must keep learning and growing every single day of your life. The potential for growth is infinite – you don't know what you are truly capable of unless you constantly keep raising the bar higher for yourself.

The Importance of a Mentor

The fastest way to go from Point A to Point B is to find someone who is already at Point B and get them to show you how they did it. Any person who is wildly successful will tell you that success is always modeled!

No one is born successful. Real success is always self-made. Of course, it's an added advantage if one is born into a wealthy family. They have the added advantage of having access to more resources. To become successful themselves, they'll still have to learn, grow, and evolve.

As Tony Robbins, one of the biggest self-help coaches of all time puts it, "Everyone needs a coach, whether it's a top-level executive, a graduate student, a homemaker, a homeless person or the President of the United States" (2012).

It doesn't matter what your goal is – if you want to be wildly successful at it, you need a mentor. By having a mentor, I am not saying that you need to sign up for one-on-one coaching. Depending upon the nature of your goals and your current financial situation, it may or may not be feasible for you. We are living in the most amazing time in history: at the click of a button, you can listen to some of the greatest minds that have ever lived.

There are many coaches who offer highly affordable, self-paced courses. You can receive coaching from books by applying what you are learning to your life. No matter what you are in life, you can't make excuses for not having a mentor when the internet has democratized education.

One-on-one coaching is still the best option. It is for people who want to perform at the highest level – those who settle for nothing but the best of the best. Working one-to-one with a mentor will bring out the very best in you that you didn't even know exists. When you feel you are giving your 100 percent, a great coach will bring out another 1 percent that you had no clue is within you.

A great mentor will push you to your limits. They will see your strengths that you haven't recognized yet. They will help you overcome your shortcomings. They will hold you accountable. They will work on your mindset and psychology. Everything in life is a mind game. If you want to become insanely wealthy, you have to first attain that goal in your mind and then it will manifest in your reality. The same goes for any goal. All battles are won first in the mind and only after that on the battlefield of life.

Having an Accountability Partner

Most people never follow through on their goals because they aren't holding themselves accountable for them. It is very easy to give up on a goal as soon as the first challenge arises when the only person to whom you are accountable is your own self. You will be a lot more likely to follow through on your promises when you are accountable to at least one more person than your own self.

Accountability breeds response-ability.

- Stephen Covey

Having an accountability partner is a game-changer. If you don't have an accountability partner right now, then you need to immediately find one for yourself.

Your ideal accountability partner would be someone with similar goals, vision, and passion. You want to establish a partnership wherein you both agree to coach and provide feedback to each other on a regular basis.

This may require you to talk daily or weekly with your accountability partner to share your wins and your challenges. It is very much like a mastermind meeting except that instead of the focus being on several people, it is only on you and your partner.

If you are wondering where and how you'll find an accountability partner, then I must say in the age of the internet you can't make excuses for not having someone like that in your life. You can very easily join an online mastermind group and ask someone from the group to be your accountability partner. Forums and social media groups focused on the topics of your interest are other great places to connect with other like-minded individuals.

Once you share your goals with your accountability partner, you want to discuss the repercussions for not following through on your commitments. For instance, if you don't wake up at 5 in the morning every day for the next week, then the consequence would be $10 for every missed day. You'll pay this amount to your partner. They can decide what consequence they want to have for not following through on their goals.

The Amateur Mental Toughness Training Program

In general, the higher the stakes, the more likely you are to follow through. Always put more at stake than less if you are truly after results. Accountability is hard to accomplish even with an accountability partner by your side when you don't have much at stake for not following through on your commitments.

Chapter Summary

- When you are approaching anything new with an attitude acquired from your past negative experience, you are pretty much setting yourself up for failure.

- The reason why people with a negative attitude fail consistently is that they are always expecting to fail. They believe that nothing good can ever happen to them. It's only a matter of time before their negative anticipation turns into a self-fulfilling prophecy.

- You can succeed at anything you set your mind to. You have to believe that it's possible and persevere until your positive expectation becomes your joyful reality.

- If your goals don't excite you and scare you, then they aren't good enough to be pursued.

- You must raise the bar for yourself. Demand nothing but excellence from yourself. Every time you think about your goals, it should fill you with excitement and a joyful sense of anticipation.

- Never allow doubts and fears to control you. Instead of wondering how or if you'll ever get there, visualize that you already have everything you are aspiring for. Allow yourself to feel happy and satisfied as though your goals have already been realized.

- To set meaningful goals, you have to first know your *why*. Your *why* is something that fuels you mentally and emotionally. It's a reason that's so strong and important that you'd stake everything you have and all that you are to get what you are after and to become who you want to be.

- Without an action plan, goals are nothing but wishes.

- An exceptional life begins with exceptional standards. With mediocre standards, you will achieve nothing more than mediocrity.

- The only difference between successful people and average people are their standards. Successful people hold themselves up to a much higher standard.

- To raise your standards, burn all your boats. As long as you have an exit strategy, you'll never hold yourself up to an exceptionally high standard.

- Success is not an isolated event that occurs out of the blue. It is the culmination point of supporting daily habits.

- While success looks glamorous, the daily grind one has to go through is far from glamorous. It's painful and repetitive. All successful people understand that success doesn't come without sweat, the daily grind, and suffering. The reason why most people will never become successful is that their primary focus is on being comfortable and avoiding pain and discomfort as much as possible.

- Successful people work harder than everyone else. They may not be the smartest, most talented, or even the cleverest; what they have is extraordinary persistence. They persevere when everyone else quits.

- According to Pareto's Principle, 80 percent of results come from 20 percent of the things that we do. You need to identify this 20 percent that will help maximize your results. Without focused goals, you will end up scattering your energy everywhere.

- One habit that most of the world's most successful people have in common is that they wake up early. They don't just attack the day in reactive mode. It's important for them to get themselves centered and grounded to face the day before the rest of the world awakes.

- You must invest time, energy, and money in taking courses, reading books, participating in masterminds, and hiring coaches.

- You shouldn't just surround yourself with people who aspire for excellence but with those from whom you can learn. You have to find a way to be in the company of individuals who inspire you. In today's times, this is easier than it has ever been in history.

- Learning is not the same as knowing things. Anyone can read a book and boast about knowing a great deal on a subject. You have never truly learned something unless you have made it completely your own.

- To live like a champion, you have to repeatedly practice your skills. Even when you gain a great deal of mastery over them, you have to continue aspiring for the next level of greatness.

- The fastest way to go from Point A to Point B is to find someone who is already at Point B and get them to show you how they did it. Any person who is wildly successful will tell you that success is always modeled!

- An accountability partner is a game-changer. If you don't have an accountability partner right now, then you need to immediately find one for yourself.

- Your ideal accountability partner would be someone with similar goals, vision, and passion. You want to establish a partnership where you both agree to coach and provide feedback to each other on a regular basis.

Chapter Seven – Pro Mental Toughness

The only way you gain mental toughness is to do things you're not happy doing. If you continue doing things that you're satisfied with and make you happy, you're not getting stronger. You're staying where you're at. Either you're getting better, or you're getting worse. You're not staying the same.

- David Goggins (Eytel, 2020)

If you have mastered the principles of the previous chapter, then you are ready to take your mental toughness training to the next level. If you haven't yet applied the teachings of the previous chapter into practice, then I would urge you to go back to the previous chapter and put into practice everything I taught you there. You don't have to do everything perfectly but you definitely need to get started. Once you have put all the learning into practice (even if it is imperfect), you are ready for the next level of mental toughness.

I want to emphasize another thing here. Developing mental toughness isn't necessarily a linear process. As you make your way through Chapters Six, Seven, and Eight, you may have to go back and work on the principles of Chapters Six and Seven even though you have made it to Chapter Eight by putting everything into practice. Putting everything into practice doesn't mean you have gained mastery over what you have learned. Developing mastery is a lifelong process and no matter how much you achieve, there will always be a next much higher level for you to aspire to.

To begin with, however, you must start in a sequence so you are gradually building up your skills. This is why I have laid out these three chapters from a beginner to an advanced level. Once you have managed to put everything into practice, you will continue to work on the different principles from all these chapters. Just because I am calling this a progression from beginner to advanced doesn't mean that the teachings of Chapters Six or Seven would become less important once you reach Chapter Eight. They are all equally important. I have simply divided them in a way that they gradually build upon one another.

You want to continue practicing all these principles not just for a few months or years but for the rest of your life. Success is a journey, not a destination. These principles are the guiding maps for your journey. Your potential for growth and success is infinite – NEVER SETTLE!

Staying Consistent - It's Easy to Start, Harder to Finish

The classic fable of the tortoise and the hare still holds true. Most people start out strong but quit as soon as the first road bump comes up. Is it surprising that the vast majority of people who buy a new annual gym membership on New Year's stop showing up after the first week! This holds true for all areas of life.

The problem is that most people do things when they 'feel like it.' Successful people don't live their life based on feelings alone. They do what needs to be done. They show up every single day – whether they feel like it or not.

Quitting is the path of least resistance. It's very easy to do. It's not surprising that most people quit when they encounter their first setback or when the going gets tough.

Success doesn't mean that you have to do what it takes for a month, a year, or even a few years. You have to show up every single day for the rest of your life because success is a never-ending journey. That one day when you didn't show up – the one day you pressed the snooze button and went back to sleep – can set you back by a few days or years.

I am not saying that you should finish every single thing you started. Indeed, there are times when you must quit, especially when you started out thinking that it is what you want but over time, realized that it's just not for you. In that case, cut your losses to preserve your time and energy. This is also why I want you to be very careful with what you are saying yes to.

You want to have clear goals – and only a few at a time. These goals should be things you desperately want. If you don't want them badly enough, you will quit too easily. Be focused. Your goals have to be clear and well-defined. When your goals are clear and well-defined, you will remain consistent in your pursuit. When you feel like quitting, you will hold on to the vision of how you see your ideal self and life. This vision will fuel you to get through the hardest of times. The more emotional appeal this vision has for you, the greater will be your motivation.

Setbacks are inevitable. There will be days when you will feel like nothing is moving. Do you know about the Chinese bamboo tree? "When you get a Chinese bamboo tree, you have to fertilize and water it every single day. Nothing happens for the first 4 years. There is no evidence that a tree will once occupy the ground on which you are watering. However, you have to remain consistent and faithful to the vision of having a Chinese bamboo tree" (Badiani, 2013). Somewhere around the fifth year, a miracle unfolds. Something begins to sprout from underneath the ground. Within a six-week period, you end up with a tree that is up to 90 feet tall. The tree can grow at a staggering rate of 48 inches per day or at a rate of 39 inches per hour. That is a truly miraculous spectacle to witness!

This is how your efforts work. You can understand success with the formula of compound interest. Initially, when the interest on the principal is being compounded, the interest is very low. Over time, as the interest is consistently compounded, the amount grows exponentially. The same is true for your efforts. While your efforts may not bear immediate results and it may even seem like nothing is working, over time, your compounded efforts will surely bear astounding results.

No successful person has ever said they will do something for a certain amount of time and then live the rest of their life basking in the glory of their achievements. They commit to what they want for however long it takes. Giving up is never an option.

Besides, who says that you will get what you want after 1 attempt, 2 attempts, 3, 4, or even 100? You have to burn your bridges, build on your experiences, and be willing to do what needs to be done for as long as it takes. No matter how many setbacks you encounter on the way, they should only fuel your drive and your passion for achieving your goals.

Every time you climb a mountain, you must find a new one to conquer. Your hunger for personal growth and for taking your life to the next level should be insatiable. Real success is not about arriving at a certain destination. It's about the person that you become while and by achieving the goals that you set for yourself. While your material achievements may leave you, the person that you have become by acquiring them will be with you forever.

Next Level Accountability and Integrity

In order to be successful, you must take full responsibility for your life. It doesn't stop there – you must live every single day of your life with complete integrity and hold yourself accountable every step of the way.

In many areas of life, responsibility can be shared but accountability and integrity can never be shared. Being accountable means you aren't just responsible for who you are, what you are experiencing, and what you are doing, you are also answerable for it.

Accountability is the courage to take ownership for all your actions – the good, the bad, and the ugly. It's the ability to admit you have made a mistake when you mess things up. It's about taking a hard look at yourself and admitting your own flaws and shortcomings.

Integrity is who you are when no one is looking. You want to keep your standards high at all times not because other people may see you but because the person inside you is always observing you.

From now on, I want you to take your practice of accountability and integrity to the next level. It is no longer enough to say that you would do something and then have the best intentions to follow through on your commitments. From now on, let there be a consequence for not following through on your commitments.

You can share the consequences with your accountability buddy. There may be certain areas of life where you are not comfortable sharing such details with anyone. You still have to hold yourself accountable because it's your self-respect that should always matter the most to you. Every time you say you would do something and don't follow through on it, you lose self-respect. So let there be a consequence for missing the mark.

For instance, if you want to work out in the morning, then make a rule for yourself that you won't have breakfast until you have worked out. You must earn your breakfast by first making your body work hard. You can decide that you will look at social media only after you have finished your work for the day. To make this easier, you can use an app that locks you out of your phone's screen for several hours. You can still receive and make calls. It's just the other features that don't work.

You must also reward yourself for all the things that you do right. After a tough workout, you can have a nice and hearty breakfast. Be careful of extremes here. You don't want to reward yourself with something unhealthy that would ruin all your efforts. After finishing work, when you finally get to social media, you can get completely sucked in and spend your entire evening and most of the night scrolling through posts. The rewards must be healthy and wholesome as much as possible. So the hearty breakfast can be something fulfilling and delicious but also healthy like some Bircher muesli and your favorite fruits. Have time limits for how long you can use social media and use it for productive purposes – to read and watch content that truly inspires you or that you can learn from.

Tunnel Vision and Single-Minded Focus

Single-minded focus is the most important prerequisite for success. You have to know what you want and you must want it bad enough to focus on it with all your might.

Where focus goes, energy flows.

Pro Mental Toughness

- Tony Robbins

What is it that you are focusing on right now? Or what is it that you aren't focusing on right now? If you want to become successful then you must become obsessed with what you want. Your goals should be the first thing you think about when you wake up and they should be the last thing on your mind as you drift into sleep every night.

Being focused on your goals means prioritizing what you want over what feels good in the moment. It means giving up distractions and replacing them with hard work and discipline.

You are the only one that can turn your dreams into reality. Without tunnel vision, you can't achieve anything worthwhile in life. You can't allow yourself to become distracted by all the other shiny objects around you or even by the opinion of naysayers. If you want something bad enough you will find a way to get there. If you can't and you still want it bad enough, you will make your own way to get there. Never let the naysayers rub their negative beliefs on you.

Stay focused no matter how distracted and distracting the world is. Dare to be the non-conformist – the weird one – the one who is more interested in doing the grind than in partying or watching seven seasons of the latest television series.

Wake up with a plan every morning and go to bed with a dream every night. Don't allow your focus to shift no matter how many challenges come up. Your vision should remain fixed on the image of you winning – whatever this may mean for you. You need to see your victory very clearly in your mind's eye and you must remain fixated with it.

People will call you obsessed – they'll brand you as a fanatic. Don't worry about it – they don't understand your standards. They don't try hard enough for anything in life so they think you are strange. Why would you even want to be one of the masses, anyway? There's nothing glorious about mediocrity. Don't let the world talk you into lowering your bar for yourself. Hold on to the vision of what you want and see nothing but it – hear nothing but it – feel nothing but it. I want you to do this night and day – obsessively, fanatically. It's that level of focus, commitment, dedication, and relentless effort that leads to extraordinary levels of success.

Affirmations

When you start feeling distracted or bogged down, practice affirmations to keep yourself focused. You can write your own. If there's a negative belief that's bothering you, you can flip it around and write the opposite. For instance, if you are afraid you will lose the match next week, you can write, "I'm easily and effortlessly winning the match."

Make sure that your affirmations are always in the present. Don't write, "I will miss the match." The mind doesn't know the difference between what is real and what is imaginary. If you can convince your mind that something is real, then it's only a matter of time before what you want becomes your immediate reality.

Here is a general affirmation that you can repeat to yourself throughout the day. Say it to yourself in the morning when you get up and repeat it as many times as possible throughout the day. You can either say it out aloud or you can repeat it silently in your mind:

I'm laser-focused on my goals. It's easy for me to get what I want. I'm a winner. All things are possible for me. I am in control of my destiny – I have the power to create the life that I want!

Meditation

This is another incredible tool that many of the world's most successful people use on a daily basis. Meditation is all about emptying your mind of the unnecessary excesses that cloud your vision and obfuscate your judgment.

You can combine meditation with visualization to make your daily practice even more powerful. I would recommend that you meditate twice a day – immediately after waking up and right before going to bed. If you think that's too much for you, then start out with meditating once a day and then gradually build your way up.

There are many ways to meditate. Here's a simple practice that you can incorporate into your daily routine:

- Step 1 – Sit down in a quiet place with your spine erect and eyes closed.

- Step 2 – Witness what is going on in your mind. Don't judge – don't try to analyze – simply observe.

- Step 3 – Focus on your breath. Notice how it is flowing through your nose and spreading through your entire body as you are taking long deep breaths. Watch the outflow of breath as your stomach and chest contract and the breath flows out of the nose. Keep your focus on the sound of the breath – notice what it feels like as it enters and leaves your nose.

- Step 4 – Practice this deep breathing by keeping the focus on your breath for as long as possible. You can start small by doing this for just 5 minutes every day and then gradually increase to 15 minutes or half an hour. There is really no upper limit – you can do it for as long as it feels right to you. The only side effects would be a calmer and more centered you.

- Step 5 – Towards the end of your meditation, invoke a vision in your mind where you see yourself achieving your goals. Watch the whole scene like a movie you are a part of. What does it feel like to be successful? What are you doing? What are you wearing? What are you saying? Make the picture as vivid as possible. You know you are doing it right when you can feel the emotions that this vision is evoking in you.

- Step 6 – Slowly move your toes and fingers. Rub your palms together and place them on your eyes. Gently open your eyes.

Conquer Your Inner Demons

Your greatest opponent is not another human – it's the voice inside your head. This voice tells you to quit when you are just getting started. When you are about to get out of bed in the morning, it says, "Let's stay in bed today – why not start tomorrow?" This voice urges you to eat that extra piece of chocolate that you know you shouldn't be eating. When you are feeling confident about your abilities, it says to you, "Who do you think you are?"

This voice mocks you, criticizes you – it makes you believe that your worst fears will come true if you keep going forward.

I am here to tell you something – this is not your voice! This voice that you think of as your own inner self has been conditioned by family, friends, and society who have transferred their own self-loathing and limiting beliefs onto you.

You don't have to choke this voice in order to conquer it. All you need to do is observe what it says without getting yourself bogged down by it. There's another voice inside you that says, "I can do it. I am capable of greatness. I deserve the best in life." The only thing you need to do is to make this voice louder than the other one.

The voice in your head that emerges as the dominant of the two determines the difference between winning and losing. If you want to win in life, then the voice of the winner must prevail inside your mind.

The solution is not to run away from your inner critic or even your greatest fears. You must sit with them. Most people are so afraid to face their inner demons that they keep constantly distracting themselves with technology. They are afraid of silence; they need constant chatter even if nothing meaningful is ever said.

I want you to get comfortable with being silent – with being alone. Go dark on all electronic stimulation for at least a few hours every day. Spend this time in contemplation and analysis – meditate on yourself and on your life. Sit in the darkness with your inner demons – what's the worst they can do to you? They lose their power over you once you stop running away from them.

Mental Resilience

Everything in life is a mind game. It doesn't matter whether you want to become an NBA champion, the vice president of your company, or the best housewife – everything is a mind game. To win in any area of life, you need to master your mindset.

There's a world outside and there's a world inside. You can't always control what's happening in the world outside but you can always control what is happening in your inner world.

Here's a short excerpt from one of the most inspiring books I have ever read, Man's Search for Meaning by Victor Frankl.

> *The salvation of man is through love and in love. I understood how a man who has nothing left in this world still may know bliss, be it only for a brief moment, in the contemplation of his beloved. In a position of utter desolation, when man cannot express himself in positive action, when his only achievement may consist in enduring his sufferings in the right way — an honourable way — in such a position man can, through loving contemplation of the image he carries of his beloved, achieve fulfilment. For the first time in my life, I was able to understand the*

meaning of the words, "The angels are lost in perpetual contemplation of an infinite glory." In front of me, a man stumbled and those following him fell on top of him. The guard rushed over and used his whip on them all. Thus my thoughts were interrupted for a few minutes. But soon my soul found its way back from the prisoner's existence to another world, and I resumed talk with my loved one: I asked her questions, and she answered; she questioned me in return, and I answered. "Stop!" We had arrived at our work site. Everybody rushed into the dark hut in the hope of getting a fairly decent tool. Each prisoner got a spade or a pickaxe. "Can't you hurry up, you pigs?" Soon we had resumed the previous day's positions in the ditch. The frozen ground cracked under the point of the pickaxes, and sparks flew. The men were silent, their brains numb. My mind still clung to the image of my wife. A thought crossed my mind: I didn't even know if she were still alive. I knew only one thing—which I have learned well by now: Love goes very far beyond the physical person of the beloved. It finds its deepest meaning in his spiritual being, his inner self. Whether or not he is actually *present, whether or not he is still alive at all, ceases somehow to be of importance. I did not know whether my wife was alive, and I had no means of finding out (during all my prison life there was no outgoing or incoming mail); but at that moment it ceased to matter (*Frankl, 2006).

These poignant passages describe Victor Frankl's life as a prisoner in a Nazi concentration camp. Even though the environment was bleak, dreary, and brutal, he managed to find joy within his inner world by contemplating that which is glorious and beautiful – in Victor Frankl's case, his wife.

It really doesn't matter what's happening around you. The only thing that truly matters is what's going on inside you. Don't let external challenges bog you down. Inside your mind, you can always have everything that you have ever wanted. As I have pointed out several times previously, the mind doesn't know the difference between what is real and what is imagined. As long as the pictures in your mind are clear and vivid enough, you will feel the emotions they evoke inside your being. That's what matters.

When you encounter setbacks and failures, keep your vision fixed on your end goal. Hold on tight and strong to the vision of what you want. If you aren't where you want to be right now, it means one thing:

This is not the end of your story. You fail only when you accept defeat so don't accept it. Let every setback strengthen your resolve to charge ahead with double the force. Cut your losses and raise yourself up – everything you want is waiting to be claimed by you. You have to believe in yourself and in what you want. Never give up – no matter how hard the going gets. You are the only one who has the power to make your dreams come true!

Chapter Summary

- Developing mastery is a lifelong process and no matter how much you achieve, there will always be a next much higher level for you to aspire to.

- Your potential for growth and success is infinite – NEVER SETTLE!

- The problem is that most people do things when they 'feel like it.' Successful people don't live their life based on feelings alone. They do what needs to be done. They show up every single day – whether they feel like it or not.

- Success doesn't mean that you have to do what it takes for a month, a year, or even a few years. You have to show up every single day for the rest of your life because success is a never-ending journey. That one day when you didn't show up – the one day you pressed the snooze button and went back to sleep – can set you back by a few days or years.

- You can understand success with the formula of compound interest. When the interest on the principal is first being compounded, the interest is very low. Over time, the interest is consistently compounded and the amount grows exponentially. The same is true for your efforts. While your efforts may not bear immediate results and it may even seem like nothing is working, over time, your compounded efforts will surely bear astounding results.

- In many areas of life, responsibility can be shared but accountability and integrity can never be shared. Being accountable means you aren't just responsible for who you are, what you are experiencing, and what you are doing, you are also answerable for it.

- Single-minded focus is the most important prerequisite for success. You have to know what you want and you must want it enough to focus on it with all your might.

- Stay focused no matter how distracted and distracting the world is. Dare to be the non-conformist – the weird one – the one who is more interested in doing the grind than in partying or watching seven seasons of the latest television series.

- Wake up with a plan every morning and go to bed with a dream every night. Don't allow your focus to shift no matter how many challenges come up.

- You can practice this affirmation every day: "I'm laser-focused on my goals. It's easy for me to get what I want. I'm a winner. All things are possible for me. I'm the master of my destiny – I have the power to create the life that I want!"

- You can combine meditation with visualization to make your daily practice even more powerful. I would recommend that you meditate twice a day – immediately after waking up and right before going to bed.

- Spend this time in contemplation and analysis – meditate on yourself and on your life. Sit in the darkness with your inner demons – what's the worst they can do to you? They lose their power over you once you stop running away from them.

- Everything in life is a mind game. It doesn't matter whether you want to become an NBA champion, the vice president of your company or the best housewife – everything is a mind game. To win in any area of life, you need to master your mindset.

- When you encounter setbacks and failures, keep your vision fixed on your end goal. Hold on to the vision of what you want. If you aren't where you want to be right now, it means just one thing: This is not the end of your story. You fail only when you accept defeat. Just don't accept it.

Chapter Eight – Elite Mental Toughness

Champions aren't made in the gyms. Champions are made from something they have deep inside them — a desire, a dream, a vision. They have to have the skill and the will. But the will must be stronger than the skill.

- Muhammad Ali

If you have come this far, I am assuming that you have already gained a certain degree of mastery over the mental toughness training we did in the previous chapters. If you feel you haven't put into practice any of the different facets of mental toughness we discussed in the previous chapters, then I would suggest going back and doing them first. Once you are ready, come back to this chapter and let us take your mental toughness training to the next level!

Mastering the Champion Mindset

The average person lives their life seeking pleasure and avoiding pain. Champions, on the other hand, understand that everything they want lies on the other end of pain and suffering. After all, nothing worthwhile can be achieved without enduring a certain amount of pain and suffering.

Jump Out of the Safety Net

Understand that your mind is there to keep you safe – it's not there to help you achieve greatness. The mind will always want to choose the path of least resistance because the mind's job is to help you survive. The world's elite understands that the mind is a terrible master but an excellent servant.

If you allow your mind to run your life, you will never achieve greatness. To achieve greatness you have to take risks, you have to do things that push you to your edge. Greatness is not something that can be found in one's comfort zone.

Don't Try to Get Anything for Free

Everyone wants to be rich, fit, healthy, and happy but very few of us are willing to pay the price for it. The masses are always looking to cut corners. They want to pay the least amount to get the maximum benefits out of life. I am not talking about payments in monetary terms.

The real payment you have to make is through sacrifice, discipline, grit, integrity, and perseverance.

I want you to get out of the mindset of getting things for free. As soon as you decide you want something, ask yourself, "What is the price I am willing to pay?"

The greater the reward you are seeking, the higher the price will be. Champions understand one thing really well – there's a time for work, and there's a time for celebration. They work relentlessly hard to get what they want and they rest only after they have achieved their goals.

Stay Hungry

Success is not a destination. It is the journey of a lifetime. No matter how far you have come, there is always another level you can achieve. For this, you need to constantly keep growing by investing in yourself (go back to Chapter Six and read again about the idea of investing in yourself – if there's just one thing you take away from this book, then I would like you to master this concept like your life depended upon it).

Never become too smug or too comfortable with where you are in life. That's when you'll become 'normal' and there's nothing spectacular or extraordinary about normalcy. If you are reading this book, I am assuming that you belong to a rare breed of humans who aren't interested in being included with the sheep in the herd.

Every day, you must raise the bar higher for yourself. If you ran 10 miles today, tomorrow you must do 12. When something starts becoming easy and too comfortable, you need to press the button and move up to the next level. Being comfortable is synonymous with being mediocre. Champions despise mediocrity. They are interested in pushing themselves to their limits.

Make a Lot of Mistakes

Most people never achieve anything worthwhile in life because they spend their entire life standing by the shore. They are too afraid to jump in the water and dive into the ocean to find the pearls that could become their destiny.

Anyone who has never made a mistake has never tried anything new.

- Albert Einstein

You can't learn anything new without first being absolutely terrible at it. You learn by making mistakes (and, of course, you can also learn from the mistakes of others).

Champions make a lot of mistakes but they learn from them and they grow. Once they become staggeringly successful at anything, it's not their failures that are remembered, it is their achievements that are glorified.

Don't Ever Let Ego Get in the Way

We discussed this in Chapter Five but it's worth repeating the importance of never letting your ego get the better of you.

Champions are always eager to learn. No matter what level of mastery they achieve in their craft, they continue to approach everything with the beginner's mind.

Normal people are more interested in looking good to others than they are in truly learning and growing. Champions don't care about the opinions of others. They know that the only person whose opinion matters is the one they're looking at in the mirror.

They admit when they don't know something instead of pretending to know the answer to everything. They are eager to learn from anyone who has something valuable to offer. It doesn't matter whether that person is significantly younger than they are or subordinate to them in the official hierarchy.

Give up the ego. Be more concerned with your personal growth and give up the desire to look good to others at your own expense.

Sherpas and Everest - Lessons from Extreme Mountaineering

While Western mountaineers are glorified, pretty much no one talks about the sherpas, the climbing guides, who accompany them on those adventures.

It's easy to idolize someone who climbs Everest as it's something that most people can only dream of. In reality, most mountaineers wouldn't even get anywhere near the summit without the help of the Sherpas who carry all the kit, the oxygen apparatus, and other necessities. These brave men regularly risk their lives to help struggling mountaineers realize their dreams.

They do it for very little money and there is no desire for fame involved. Their primary motivation is to earn an honest living to feed their families.

Most of these climbing guides come from an ethnic group that's known as the Sherpa people. Hence, Sherpa is both a term used in the Himalayas to refer to a climbing guide and also the ethnic group to which most of them belong.

The Sherpa people are renowned for their superior strength, outstanding endurance, and excellent climbing skills at high altitudes. Despite their reputation, they aren't glorified in the media in the same way as western mountaineers who climb Everest are.

Most of these sherpas live humble lives working in dangerous conditions. While you get to hear about the tourists who died facing massive avalanches and other extreme adverse situations on their way to the summit, the stories of these sherpas are hardly ever highlighted.

As Kami Rita Sherpa, a world record holder for having been on top of Everest more times than anyone else, puts it, "Without a Sherpa, there is no expedition"(Bashyal, 2019).

Truth be told, without the help of the sherpas, most Western tourists would not even dare to venture on such hostile territory.

It's clear from Kami's statements made to the BBC (Bashyal, 2019), it's not fame or glory that he was seeking. To him, the greatest reward lies in being able to help tourists fulfill their dream. The fact that he became a world record holder for reaching the summit of Mount Everest more times than anyone else is simply a by-product of his passion and genuine desire to help others fulfill their dreams.

Sherpas are also known for their cheerful and jovial nature. Even after a hard day of toil, they manage to retain a smile on their face and attack any other challenging task that may come up with the same infectious cheerfulness (Robertson, 2021).

There's a lot we can learn from the sherpas and their attitude towards life. Indeed, life is extremely tough and challenging in the remote Himalayas but with their attitude, sherpas have learned to make the most of what they have. They genuinely care about helping tourists while making an honest living. For them, climbing mount Everest is an everyday activity – not that it isn't challenging or excruciating for them. Since that's their means for earning a livelihood, they give their best and are willing to regularly risk their lives for it.

Being a champion doesn't mean you have to be recognized as one by the world. A real champion is one who knows deep inside that they are giving their all every single day. The only person whose respect and admiration you need to earn is yours.

Do your best every day. Maybe you will end up with a world record like Kami or maybe you won't. The most important thing is to go to bed every night knowing you gave your absolute best and tomorrow you will wake up again to do the same!

Small Changes Lead to Huge Transformations

When people think about changing something, they immediately think of a huge transformation. They want to go from Point A to Point D without having to encounter Point B and C along the way. Most of the time, people's attempts to change their life fail because their plans are overambitious for their current situation and capability.

For instance, if a 300-pound person decides that they'll work out 7 hours a day and lose all the excess weight in 2 months, it's inevitable that this plan would fail, especially if they haven't set foot in the gym in years. While they may be able to get themselves to work out for 7 hours for a few days, they won't be able to carry on with such a schedule as it is likely going to be incompatible with their current physical stamina and lifestyle.

To achieve macro-level transformation, changes have to be made at the micro level. For that person, it may be better to go for a 15-minute walk on the first day and then slowly work their way up to a half an hour workout in a week or two. Intense sporadic actions hardly ever lead to massive changes. Transformation occurs only with consistent regular effort.

When Dave Brailsford was hired as the performance director for overseeing the training and performance of the British cycling team that was to participate in the Olympics, the team was in really bad shape. People expected nothing but the worst performance from the team and the idea of winning at the Olympics seemed nothing more than a chimera (Clear, 2020).

Brailsford and his coaches, however, revolutionized the training program. Instead of making big dramatic changes, Brailsford and his coaches focused on figuring out how they could make just 1 percent improvement in a particular area. They applied this 1 percent improvement rule to even the smallest of details – like finding the ideal pillow and mattress to help the riders get a restful night's sleep or providing them with a massage gel that would slightly improve muscle recovery.

Over time, the small changes compounded to bring about a massive transformation. The British cycling team won many gold medals at the 2008 Olympic games. British cyclists have won many medals on the international stage since then.

If you want to change your life, don't attempt to take a leap. Instead, take small baby steps every single day. At first, it will seem like you aren't making much progress. Trust me, over time, your consistent marginal improvements will bear fruit.

The Art of Stoicism and Non-Attachment

This is one of the most important things you must master. Do your best but let go of your attachment to the outcome. Most people give up because they are way too attached to the outcome. They go to the gym for one or two days and then quit because they can't see any significant change in their body.

You know you are a real champion when you are willing to do whatever it takes for however long it takes. You have a vision for how you would like everything to turn out but you are not attached to how or when it will happen. You are secure in your faith and self-confidence that what you want is already yours. It is only a matter of time before your vision will manifest itself in material reality.

Things are as they are. Looking out into the universe at night, we make no comparisons between right and wrong stars, nor between well and badly arranged constellations.

- Alan Watts *(*Arvide, 2018)

Another thing I want to caution you about is to have the most rigorous standards only for yourself and not for others. If you start demanding that your loved ones and other people close to you live by the same standards, you'll encounter disappointment. As Marcus Aurelius said, "Be tolerant with others and strict with yourself."

Be grateful for the people in your life but be cautious not to see them as extensions of your own self, just like how you wouldn't like them to see you as an extension of their own self. Because they are close to you doesn't mean that they have to be like you. You can love people while being different from them and respecting the fact that they may not have the same kind of standards for themselves as you have for you.

Apart from this, make sure that you are able to keep yourself calm through the different seasons of life. Mastering the art of self-control is the key to success. You must discipline your thoughts and your emotions. Don't let them run the show. While having an emotional outburst may feel relieving at the moment, it is likely to leave you with regrets and guilt.

Channel your emotions through exercise, journaling, meditation, affirmations, and other such self-help practices.

When things are going rough, hold on to the vision of what you want and keep on believing that it is already yours. The storm will pass and you will find yourself on a new shore and it would likely be the one you had been dreaming of arriving at for a very long time.

Always remember this life is just an experience. We are all here to learn and grow. Give your best, do your best but don't fret too much. Savor each experience and learn from it.

Bill Hicks, the legendary stand-up comedian says it perfectly:

The world is like a ride in an amusement park. And when you choose to go on it you think it's real because that's how powerful our minds are. And the ride goes up and down and round and round. It has thrills and chills and it's very brightly colored and it's very loud and it's fun, for a while. Some people have been on the ride for a long time and they begin to question: "Is this real, or is this just a ride?" And other people have remembered, and they come back to us, they say: "Hey, don't worry, don't be afraid, ever, because this is just a ride."

Chapter Summary

- The average person lives their life seeking pleasure and avoiding pain. Champions, on the other hand, understand that everything they want lies on the other end of pain and suffering. After all, nothing worthwhile can be achieved without enduring a certain amount of pain and suffering.

- The mind will always want to choose the path of least resistance because the mind's job is to help you survive. If you allow your mind to run your life, you will never achieve greatness. To achieve greatness you have to take risks, you have to do things that push you to your edge. Greatness is not something that can be found in one's comfort zone.

Elite Mental Toughness

- The greater the reward you are seeking, the higher will be the price.

- The real payment you have to make is through sacrifices, discipline, grit, integrity, and perseverance.

- Success is not a destination. It is the journey of a lifetime. No matter how far you have come, there is always another level you can achieve. Constantly keep growing by investing in yourself.

- You can't learn anything new without first being absolutely terrible at it. You learn by making mistakes (and, of course, also learn from the mistakes of others). Champions make a lot of mistakes but they learn from them and they grow.

- Normal people are more interested in looking good to others than they are in truly learning and growing. Champions don't care about the opinions of others. They know that the only person whose opinion matters is the one looking at them in the mirror.

- Being a champion doesn't mean you have to be recognized as one by the world. A real champion is one who knows deep inside that they are giving their all every single day of their life.

- The most important thing is to go to bed every night knowing you gave your absolute best and tomorrow you will wake up again to do the same.

- To achieve macro-level transformation, changes have to be made at the micro level. Over time, the small changes compound to bring about a massive transformation.

- To change your life, don't attempt to take a giant leap. Instead, take small baby steps every single day. At first, it will seem like you aren't making much progress but, over time, your consistent marginal improvements will bear fruit.

- Do your best but let go of your attachment to the outcome. Most people give up because they are way too attached to the outcome.

- You know you are a real champion when you are willing to do whatever it takes for however long it takes. You have a vision for how you would like everything to turn out but you are not attached to how or when it will happen. You are secure in your faith and self-confidence that what you want is already yours. It is only a matter of time that your vision will manifest itself in material reality.

- You can love people while being different from them and respecting the fact that they may not have the same kind of standards for themselves as you have for you.

- When things are going rough, hold on to the vision of what you want and keep on believing that it is already yours. One day, the storm will pass and you will find yourself on a new shore and it will likely be the one you had been dreaming of arriving at for a very long time.

Conclusion

I want to thank you for putting your trust in me on this journey of building mental toughness. Even though we have reached the end of the book, your work has just begun. Building mental toughness is an endeavor of a lifetime. No matter how far you have come, you can always go further. You don't know what you are capable of until you keep pushing your boundaries. I urge you to constantly keep raising the bar higher for yourself.

Don't ever sit on your laurels for too long. As soon as you achieve something, find a new goal that you're excited to accomplish. I am not saying that you shouldn't celebrate your wins. Of course, you should regularly reward yourself for all your hard work. I am cautioning you from becoming complacent as that's a surefire way to slip into the box of mediocrity.

As I stated in Chapter Eight, if there's one thing you take away from this book, let it be the concept of investing in yourself. Make sure

Conclusion

that you are constantly investing time, money, and energy into bettering yourself in every way possible. Your goal should always be to become a better-than-the-best version of yourself.

In your pursuit of greatness, never compare yourself with anyone else. Everyone has their own journey – you can never fully understand what someone else's life is truly like. Your only competition should be the person who looks back at you in the mirror.

Don't ever wait for motivation to strike you. You have got to do what must be done every single day whether you are in the mood for it or not. This is the only way to discipline your mind and emotions. Most people are not successful because they don't do what needs to be done, they do what they are feeling like doing at the moment. As I said earlier, the mind is a terrible master. You have to take the reins and show your mind who the boss really is!

Like the vast majority of people do, don't let short-term pleasures distract you from your long-term goals. While it feels more comfortable to sit on the couch watching TV and eating fries, it hurts your long-term self-esteem. This kind of pleasure leaves you with guilt and self-loathing. Of course, since you have read this book, I am assuming you are the type of person to whom such things hardly ever happen. But you can't ever let your guard down. It's very easy to slip. We all know that after having the first bar of chocolate it's a lot harder to stop than if you never took that bite in the first place.

Practice tough love on yourself. Get yourself to do things that you absolutely hate doing or those things that truly scare you. You will feel terrible while doing it but once you are finished, your self-esteem will rise stupendously. You want to always be proud of yourself and for that, you have to get yourself to do the things that challenge and scare you. You earn your own respect every time you conquer your limitations.

This also means having the courage to stand for your own truth and your own values even when no one else believes in them or in you. You must be okay with being disliked. Champions don't live their lives to please others. They are motivated by an insatiable hunger to live a limitless life and to explore those aspects of the human experience that will remain forever elusive to the masses.

Mediocrity is easy – anyone can do it. Greatness is the prerogative of the select few who dare to venture where the masses won't dare set foot. This doesn't mean that the potential for greatness isn't present in everyone. The tragedy is that in most people it remains dormant forever as they are too smug or too scared and are living a life of least resistance.

Conclusion

Before you close this book, I want to remind you that greatness is a choice – it is not a choice that you make once in a lifetime. It is a choice that you make every single moment of every day. Mediocrity is always one choice away. You can't ever allow your standards to drop. Every day, the bar must be raised to another level. Wake up every morning with passion and excitement to grind the day. Resolve that no matter what comes up, you will emerge victorious. Friedrich Nietzsche was on to something when he said, "Out of life's school of war — what doesn't kill me, makes me stronger" (n.d.).

Don't let this book become something you read only once. Treat this as your manual for building mental toughness. Keep coming back to it every now and then. In fact, I would recommend that you read a few pages or even just a few paragraphs every single day. Now that you have read the entire book, you don't necessarily have to re-read everything in a sequential manner.

I would advise that you randomly pull any page and read whatever catches your eye. You can also browse through the table of contents and pick out a topic that catches your fancy on that particular day and read it. You don't need to read the entire chapter if you don't want to. Just read a few paragraphs and then mull over it. It's not how much you are reading that matters but how much you are understanding, assimilating, and practicing in your own life.

The more frequently you practice the principles I have laid down in this book, the more mental toughness you would build. As I said earlier, it is the journey of a lifetime because growth and the potential for self-improvement are truly infinite!

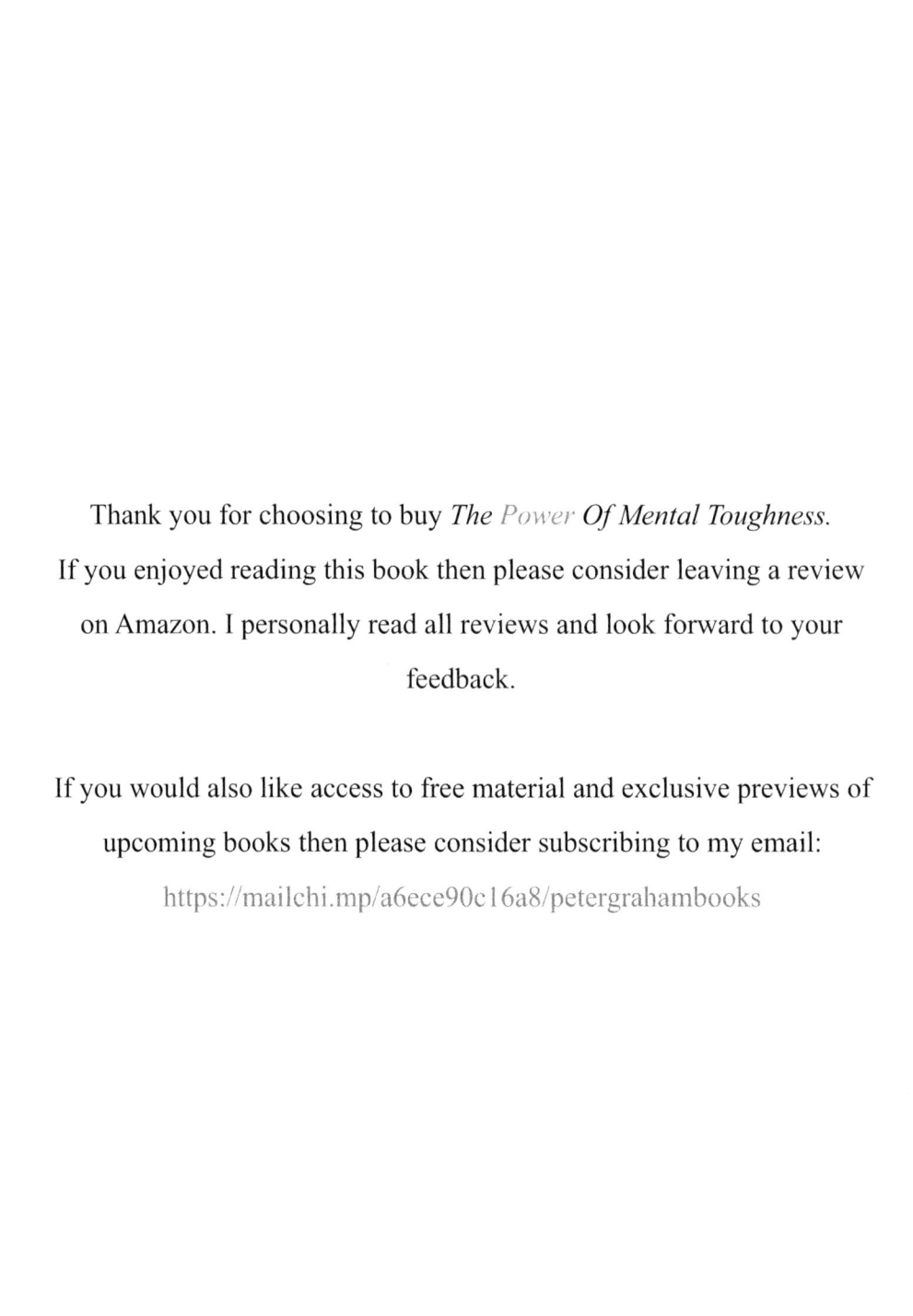

Thank you for choosing to buy *The Power Of Mental Toughness.* If you enjoyed reading this book then please consider leaving a review on Amazon. I personally read all reviews and look forward to your feedback.

If you would also like access to free material and exclusive previews of upcoming books then please consider subscribing to my email: https://mailchi.mp/a6ece90c16a8/petergrahambooks

References

6 Stories of Super Successes Who Overcame Failure. (2014, December 8). Entrepreneur. Retrieved August 13, 2021, from https://www.entrepreneur.com/article/240492

10 Life Lessons from Vince Lombardi. (2016, October 13). Fearless Motivation. Retrieved August 10, 2021, from https://www.fearlessmotivation.com/2016/01/13/10-lessons-vince-lombardi/

Amabile, T., & Kramer, S. (2011). *The Progress Principle.* Reed Business Education.

Angelou, M. (n.d.). *A quote by Maya Angelou.* Goodreads. Retrieved August 3, 2021, from https://www.goodreads.com/quotes/3759-courage-is-the-most-important-of-all-the-virtues-because

Armstrong, L. (n.d.). *Lance Armstrong Quotes.* BrainyQuote. Retrieved August 3, 2021, from https://www.brainyquote.com/quotes/lance_armstrong_193138

Attitude (psychology). (2021, July 30). Wikipedia. Retrieved July 27, 2021, from https://en.wikipedia.org/wiki/Attitude_(psychology)

Arvide, J. A. (2018, January 10). *11 Quotes From Alan Watts That Will Change Your Life.* Lifehack. Retrieved July 28, 2021, from https://

References

www.lifehack.org/articles/communication/11-quotes-from-alan-watts-that-will-change-your-life.html

Ashe, A. (n.d.). *Arthur Ashe Quotes*. BrainyQuote. Retrieved August 3, 2021, from https://www.brainyquote.com/quotes/arthur_ashe_109755

Bashyal, B. P. (2019, June 8). *Everest through the eyes of a Sherpa: Climbers need to wake up*. BBC News. https://www.bbc.com/news/world-asia-48464030

Badiani, V. (2013, April 7). *Learning from the Chinese bamboo tree*. Futurpreneur Canada. https://www.futurpreneur.ca/en/2012/chinese-bamboo-tree/

Be Tough On Yourself and Understanding To Others. Daily Stoic: Ancient Wisdom for Everyday Life. Retrieved August 12, 2021, from https://dailystoic.com/tough-understanding-others/

Bornstein, A. (2021, March 13). *8 Lessons From Arnold Schwarzenegger For Personal Success*. Born Fitness. https://www.bornfitness.com/8-lessons-arnold-schwarzenegger-success/

Brown, Les. (1998). *It's Not Over Until You Win: How to Become the Person You Always Wanted to Be No Matter What the Obstacle*. Simon & Schuster.

Christian, J. (2018, February 16). *How to Build Self-Confidence.* Medium. Retrieved August 15, 2021, from https://jessichristian.medium.com/how-to-build-self-confidence-7ba7fd15786e

Churchill, W. (n.d.). *Winston Churchill Quotes.* Brainy Quote. Retrieved August 10, 2021, from https://www.brainyquote.com/quotes/winston_churchill_124653

Clear, J. (2014, March 26). *Don't Wait for Motivation. Do This Instead.* Entrepreneur. Retrieved August 15, 2021, from https://www.entrepreneur.com/article/232349

Clear, J. (2020, February 4). *Marginal Gains: This Coach Improved Every Tiny Thing by 1 Percent.* James Clear. https://jamesclear.com/marginal-gains

Cobain, K. (n.d.). *Kurt Cobain Quotes.* Goodreads. Retrieved August 10, 2021, from https://www.goodreads.com/quotes/830628-they-laugh-at-me-because-i-m-different-i-laugh-at

Coelho, P. (1993). *The Alchemist.* HarperCollins.

Confucius. (n.d.). *Quote by Confucius.* Goodreads. Retrieved August 3, 2021, from https://www.goodreads.com/quotes/7854941-if-you-are-the-smartest-person-in-the-room-then

References

Covey, S. (n.d.). *Stephen Covey Quotes.* BrainyQuote. Retrieved August 3, 2021, from https://www.brainyquote.com/quotes/stephen_covey_636497

Einstein, A. (n.d.). *Albert Einstein Quotes.* BrainyQuote. Retrieved August 3, 2021, from https://www.brainyquote.com/quotes/albert_einstein_109012

Elrod, H. (2012). *The Miracle Morning: The Not-So-Obvious Secret Guaranteed to Transform Your Life (Before 8AM).* Hal Elrod; 1st Paperback Edition. https://miraclemorning.com

Experts Teach Why You Need Goals in Life. (2017, April 23). Fearless Motivation. Retrieved August 4, 2021, from https://www.fearlessmotivation.com/2017/04/03/need-goals-in-life/

Eytel, C. (2020, February 2). *Psychology of Winning: Mental Toughness.* National Scouting Report. Retrieved July 30, 2021, from https://www.nsr-inc.com/scouting-news/psychology-winning-mental-toughness/

Ferris, T. (2007). *The Four Day Workweek.* Harmony. https://fourhourworkweek.com

Frankl, V. E. (2006). *Man's Search for Meaning.* Amsterdam University Press.

Gluskin, D. (n.d.). *Dawn Gluskin Quotes*. Goodreads. Retrieved August 3, 2021, from https://www.goodreads.com/quotes/1357934-don-t-take-life-too-seriously-nobody-gets-out-alive-anyway

Hansen, M. V., & Allen, R. G. (2002). *The One Minute Millionaire: The Enlightened Way to Wealth*. Crown Business.

Hicks, B. (n.d.) *Life is Just a Ride.* Genius. Retrieved August 14, 2021, from https://genius.com/Bill-hicks-life-is-just-a-ride-annotated

Holtz, L. (n.d.). *Lou Holtz Quotes*. BrainyQuote. Retrieved August 3, 2021, from https://www.brainyquote.com/quotes/lou_holtz_653835#:%7E:text=Lou%20Holtz%20Quotes&text=Please%20enable%20Javascript-,Winners%20embrace%20hard%20work.,And%20that's%20the%20difference

Jordan, M. (n.d.). *Michael Jordan Quotes*. BrainyQuote. Retrieved August 3, 2021, from https://www.brainyquote.com/quotes/michael_jordan_127660#:%7E:text=Michael%20Jordan%20Quotes&text=I've%20missed%20more%20than%209000%20shots%20in%20my%20career,over%20again%20in%20my%20life

Kidd, C., Palmeri, H., Aslin, R. (2012). *Rational snacking: Young children's decision-making on the marshmallow task is moderated*

References

by beliefs about environmental reliability. Cognition. DOI: 10.1016/j.cognition.2012.08.004

King Jr., M. L. (n.d.). *Martin Luther King, Jr. Quotes*. BrainyQuote. Retrieved August 3, 2021, from https://www.brainyquote.com/quotes/martin_luther_king_jr_101378

Kiyosaki, R.T. (2007). *Rich Dad, Poor Dad*. Time Warner Books UK.

Lee, B. (n.d.). *A quote by Bruce Lee*. Goodreads. Retrieved August 5, 2021, from https://www.goodreads.com/quotes/4146-do-not-pray-for-an-easy-life-pray-for-the

Logan, P. (2019, March 4). *The Commando Values: The Importance of Ethos, Culture & Psychological Wellbeing for Optimal Performance, Part 2 of 3*. L&M Performance Psychology for Business and Sport. Retrieved August 14, 2021, from https://www.landmconsulting.co.uk/2019/03/04/the-importance-of-ethos-culture-psychological-wellbeing-for-optimal-performance-part-2-of-3/

Logan, P. (2019, March 4). *The Commando Values: The Importance of Ethos, Culture & Psychological Wellbeing for Optimal Performance, Part 3 of 3*. L&M Performance Psychology for Business and Sport. Retrieved August 14, 2021, from https://www.landmconsulting.co.uk/2019/03/04/the-importance-of-ethos-culture-psychological-wellbeing-for-optimal-performance-part-3-of-3/

Maraboli, S. (2013). *Unapologetically You: Reflections on Life and the Human Experience.* A Better Today.

McDonald, G. (2018, Jan 18). *Royal Marines slang: 27 phrases that only make sense to bootnecks.* The Plymouth Herald. Retrieved August 14, 2021, from https://www.plymouthherald.co.uk/news/plymouth-news/royal-marines-slang-27-phrases-1091118

McNee, L. (2021, July 15). *10 Famous Artists Who Had to Deal with Rejection During Their Lifetime.* Lori McNee - Fine Art & Tips. https://lorimcnee.com/10-famous-artists-who-died-before-their-art-was-recognized/

McRaven, A. W. H. (2014, May 16). *Adm. McRaven Urges Graduates to Find Courage to Change the World.* UT News. https://news.utexas.edu/2014/05/16/mcraven-urges-graduates-to-find-courage-to-change-the-world/

Nietzsche, F. (n.d.). *Friedrich Nietzsche Quotes.* BrainyQuote. Retrieved August 3, 2021, from https://www.brainyquote.com/quotes/friedrich_nietzsche_101616

References

Proctor, B. (n.d.). Bob Proctor Quotes. Goodreads. Retrieved August 3, 2021, from https://www.goodreads.com/quotes/4473051-most-people-are-not-going-after-what-they-want-even

Robbins, T. (2012). *Awaken the Giant Within*. Simon & Schuster.

Robbins, T. (n.d.). *Where Focus Goes, Energy Flows*. Tony Robbins. Retrieved July 30, 2021, from https://www.tonyrobbins.com/career-business/where-focus-goes-energy-flows/

Robertson, T. (2021, May 29). *Why are Sherpas always happy?* Nepali Times. https://www.nepalitimes.com/here-now/why-are-sherpas-always-happy/

Rohn, J. (n.d.-a). *A quote by Jim Rohn*. Goodreads. Retrieved August 3, 2021, from https://www.goodreads.com/quotes/178382-success-is-nothing-more-than-a-few-simple-disciplines-practiced

Rohn, J. (n.d.). *Jim Rohn Quotes*. Goodreads. Retrieved August 3, 2021, from https://www.goodreads.com/quotes/1798-you-are-the-average-of-the-five-people-you-spend

Rowling, J.K. (2008, June 8.) *Text of J.K. Rowling's speech*. The Harvard Gazette. https://news.harvard.edu/gazette/story/2008/06/text-of-j-k-rowling-speech/

The Royal Marines Charity. (n.d.). *The Royal Marines Charity*. https://

rma-trmc.org/our-vision/

Silva, J. (2021, June 7). *No Excuses by Brian Tracy Summary.* Jeremy Silva. Retrieved August 2, 2021, from https://jsilva.blog/2021/06/07/no-excuses-by-brian-tracy-summary/

Stanford marshmallow experiment. (2021, June 19). in Wikipedia. Retrieved July 30, 2021, from https://en.wikipedia.org/wiki/Stanford_marshmallow_experiment

Swindoll, C. (n.d.). Charles R. Swindoll Quotes. Goodreads. Retrieved August 15, 2021, from https://www.goodreads.com/author/quotes/5139.Charles_R_Swindoll

Tredgold, G. (n.d.). *50 Inspirational Pieces of Wisdom From Muhammad Ali.* Inc. Retrieved July 28, 2021, from https://www.inc.com/gordon-tredgold/muhammad-ali-50-inspiring-thoughts-from-the-greatest-of-all-time.html

Printed in Great Britain
by Amazon